INFORMATION SECURITY RISK MANAGEMENT FOR ISO27001 / ISO27002

Information Security Risk Management for ISO27001 / ISO27002

ALAN CALDER

STEVE G WATKINS

IT Governance Publishing

Every possible effort has been made to ensure that the information contained in this book is accurate at the time of going to press, and the publishers and the author cannot accept responsibility for any errors or omissions, however caused. No responsibility for loss or damage occasioned to any person acting, or refraining from action, as a result of the material in this publication can be accepted by the publisher or the author.

Apart from any fair dealing for the purposes of research or private study, or criticism or review, as permitted under the Copyright, Designs and Patents Act 1988, this publication may only be reproduced, stored or transmitted, in any form, or by any means, with the prior permission in writing of the publisher or, in the case of reprographic reproduction, in accordance with the terms of licences issued by the Copyright Licensing Agency. Enquiries concerning reproduction outside those terms should be sent to the publishers at the following address:

IT Governance Publishing
IT Governance Limited
Unit 3, Clive Court
Bartholomew's Walk
Cambridgeshire Business Park
Ely
Cambridgeshire
CB7 4EH
United Kingdom

www.itgovernance.co.uk

The authors have asserted the rights of the author under the Copyright, Designs and Patents Act, 1988, to be identified as the authors of this work.

First published in the United Kingdom in 2007 (as *Information Security Risk Management for ISO27001 / ISO17799*) by IT Governance Publishing.

ISBN 978-1-84928-043-3 this edition
ISBN 978-1-905356-23-2 original edition

ABOUT THE AUTHORS

Alan Calder is the founder director of IT Governance Ltd (*www.itgovernance.co.uk*), an information, advice and consultancy firm that helps companies tackle governance, risk management, compliance and information security issues. He has many years of senior management and board-level experience in the private and public sectors. The company's website is a 'one-stop-shop' for information, books, tools, training and consultancy on governance, risk management, compliance and information security.

Steve G Watkins leads the consultancy and training services of IT Governance Ltd. In his various roles in both the public and private sectors, he has been responsible for most support disciplines. He has over 20 years' experience of managing integrated management systems, including maintenance of information security, quality, environmental and Investors in People certifications. As well as being a lead auditor for ISO27001 and ISO9000, Steve is a trained EFQM assessor and holds diplomas in safety and financial management. He is Chair of the ISO/IEC 27001 User Group, the UK Chapter of the ISMS International User Group and was recently invited to become, and is now, an ISMS Technical Expert for UKAS, advising on their assessments of certification bodies offering ISO27001 accredited certification. Steve sits on the Management Committee of the British Standards Society where he chairs the Corporate Governance Group and is an active member of the committee responsible for writing BS31100, the British Standard for Risk Management (Code of Practice).

About the Authors

Alan Calder and Steve G Watkins have written a number of other books together, including:

- *IT Governance: A Manager's Guide to Data Security and ISO 27001/ISO 27002* (fourth edition published by Kogan Page, 2007)
- *International IT Governance: An Executive Guide to ISO 17799/ISO 27001* (published by Kogan Page, 2006)
- *ISO27001 and Information Security: A Glossary* (published by ITGP, 2010).

A list of all their publications can be found at the back of this book.

CONTENTS

Contents

Contents

x

INTRODUCTION

In today's information economy, the development, exploitation and protection of information assets are key to the long-term competitiveness and survival of corporations and entire economies. The protection of information assets – information security – is therefore overtaking physical asset protection as a fundamental corporate governance responsibility. Information security management, defined as 'the protection of information from a wide range of threats in order to ensure business continuity, minimize business risk, and maximize return on investments and business opportunities',[1] is becoming a critical corporate discipline, alongside marketing, sales, HR and financial management.

A key corporate governance objective is to ensure that the organisation has an appropriate balance of risk and reward in its business operations and, as a consequence, enterprise risk management (ERM) increasingly provides a framework within which organisations can assess and manage risks in their business plan. The recognition of substantial, strategic risk in information and communication technologies has led to the development of IT governance.[2]

The changing global economy, together with recent corporate and IT governance developments, all provide the context within which organisations have to assess risks to the information assets on which their organisations, and the

---

[1] ISO/IEC 27002:2005, clause 0.1 'What is information security?'
[2] Other books by the same authors discuss these issues in greater detail. See, for instance, *International IT Governance: An Executive Guide to ISO 27001/ISO 17799* (Kogan Page, 2006).

delivery of their business plan objectives, depend. Information security management decisions are entirely driven by specific decisions made as an outcome of a risk assessment process in relation to identified risks and specific information assets.

Risk assessment is, therefore, the core competence of information security management.

The early clauses of ISO/IEC 27002:2005 (ISO27002), the international code of best practice for information security management systems, support this business- and risk-oriented approach. Information security requirements should be 'identified by a methodical assessment of security risks. Expenditure on controls needs to be balanced against the business harm likely to result from security failures'.[3]

A growing number of organisations are adopting this approach to the management of risk. A number of national or proprietary standards that deal with information security risk management have emerged over the last few years. They all have much in common. ISO27001 is the international standard for information security management and provides an approach to risk management which is consistent with all other guidance. This approach is also appropriate for organisations complying with the PCI DSS.[4]

Of course, every organisation needs to determine its criteria for accepting risks, and identify the levels of risk it will accept. It is a truism to point out that there is a relationship

---

[3] ISO/IEC 27002:2005, clause 0.4 'Assessing security risks'.
[4] Payment Card Industry Data Security Standard, in version 1.2 at the time this book was published.

between the levels of risk and reward in any business. Most businesses, particularly those subject to the Sarbanes-Oxley Act of 2002 and, in the UK, the Turnbull Guidance within the Combined Code on Corporate Governance, will want to be very clear about which risks they will accept and which they won't, the extent to which they will accept risks and how they wish to control them. Management needs to specify its approach, in general and in particular, so that the business can be managed within that context. As we have already indicated, risk assessment, as an activity, should be approached within the context of the organisation's broader enterprise risk management (ERM) framework.

Whilst ISO27002 is a code of practice, ISO/IEC 27001:2005 (ISO27001) is a specification that sets out the requirements for an information security management system (ISMS). ISO27001 is explicit in requiring a risk assessment to be carried out before any controls[5] are selected and implemented, and is equally explicit that the selection of every control must be justified by a risk assessment. Risk assessment, as we've already said, is therefore, the core competence of information security management.

Organisations that design and implement an ISMS in line with the specification of ISO27001 can have it assessed by a third party certification body and if, after audit, it is found to be in line with ISO27001, an accredited certificate of conformity can be issued.[6]

---

[5] A 'control' can be thought of as a countermeasure, or mitigation, for a risk. See *A Dictionary of Information Security Terms, Abbreviations and Acronyms* (ITGP, 2007).
[6] There is a full description of the process of accredited certification in *IT Governance: A Manager's Guide to Data Security and ISO 27001/ISO 27002* by Alan Calder and Steve Watkins (Kogan Page, 2008).

Introduction

This standard is increasingly seen as offering a practical solution to the growing range of information-related regulatory requirements, as well as helping organisations to more cost-effectively counter the increasingly sophisticated and varied range of information security threats in the modern information economy.[7] As a result, a rapidly growing number of companies around the world are seeking certification to ISO27001.

An ISMS developed and based on risk acceptance/rejection criteria, and using third party accredited certification to provide an independent verification of the level of assurance, is an extremely useful management tool. Such an ISMS offers the opportunity to define and monitor service levels internally, as well as in contractor/partner organisations, thus demonstrating the extent to which there is effective control of those risks for which directors and senior management are accountable.

It is becoming increasingly common for ISO27001 certification to be a pre-requisite in service specification procurement documents and, as buyers become more sophisticated in their understanding of the ISO27001 accredited certification scheme, so they will increasingly set out their requirements more specifically, not only in terms of certification itself, but also in respect to the scope of the certification and the level of assurance they require. This rapid maturing in the understanding of buyers, as they seek greater assurance from an accredited certification to ISO27001, is driving organisations to improve the quality

---

[7] See *The Case for ISO 27001* by Alan Calder (ITGP, 2005) for detailed coverage of the business, contractual and regulatory reasons that should lead an organisation to consider developing an ISMS in line with the ISO27001 specification.

of their ISMS and, by definition, to improve the granularity and accuracy of their risk assessments.

The level of assurance relates, of course, directly to the risk assessment and management aspects of creating and maintaining an ISO27001-compliant ISMS. It is this key aspect that ensures that a consistent level of assurance is achieved across all facets of information security within an organisation.

ISO27001 is a specification for an ISMS. As we have said, it is based on risk assessment, both initially and on an ongoing basis. ISO27001 goes so far as to specify the steps that an information security risk assessment must go through, and the level of granularity required of it. While there are many recognised – and valid – approaches to risk assessment, an organisation that wishes to achieve ISO27001 certification must meet the requirements set out in the standard itself. There is no room for half measures: either a risk assessment methodology is in line with the requirements of ISO27001, in which case accredited certification is within reach, or it is not, in which case accredited certification is not going to happen.

This book has been written to expand on guidance that is already contained within other ISO27001 implementation books[8] by the same authors. It draws on emerging national and international best practice around risk assessment, including ISO/IEC 27005:2008 (ISO27005). It has been written to provide detailed and practical guidance to

---

[8] See, in particular, *IT Governance: A Manager's Guide to Data Security and ISO 27001/ISO 27002* (Kogan Page, 2008) and *International IT Governance: An Executive Guide to ISO 27001/ISO 17799* (Kogan Page, 2006). Note also the range of ISO27001 implementation guidance titles listed in the resources section at the back of the book.

information security and risk management teams on how to develop and implement a risk assessment and risk management process that will be in line with the requirements of ISO27001, that will reflect the best practice guidance of ISO27005, and which will simultaneously deliver real, bottom-line, business benefits.

CHAPTER 1: RISK MANAGEMENT[9]

'Risk', says NIST,[10] is the 'net negative impact of the exercise of a vulnerability, considering both the probability and the impact of occurrence'.[11] ISO27001, the international information security standard, doesn't define risk, although it does provide definitions for the whole range of risk-related activities. ISO/IEC 27000:2009 *Information Security Management Systems – Overview and Vocabulary* (ISO27000) defines risk in the same way as does ISO Guide 73:2002,[12] which is that risk is the 'combination of the probability of an event and its occurrence'.

The NIST definition of risk is in line with that used in ISO27000, and is the first indicator that a risk assessment that will meet the requirements of ISO27001 will also be in line with the NIST recommendations. ISO27005 defines information security risk as the 'potential that a given threat will exploit vulnerabilities of an asset or group of assets and thereby cause harm to the organization', and ISO27001 follows this definition.

---

[9] Some of this chapter replicates (but does not replace) material that is already in *IT Governance: A Manager's Guide to Data Security and ISO 27001/ISO 27002* (Kogan Page, 2008), as well as *International IT Governance: an Executive Guide to ISO 27001/ISO 17799* (Kogan Page, 2006), and is repeated here to provide the top-level context for the further, more detailed, contents of this book. Readers are encouraged to read the original books for the full value of the overall guidance on planning and executing an ISO27001 project.

[10] The National Institute of Standards and Technology is the US Federal Agency that develops and promotes measurement, standards and technology.

[11] NIST SP 800-30.

[12] ISO/IEC Guide 73:2002, *Risk Management – Vocabulary – Guidelines for use in standards*.

All organisations face risks of one sort or another on a daily basis and ISO27001 expects that an organisation's information security management policy will align with 'the organization's strategic risk management context'[13]. It is therefore appropriate to consider, briefly, the organisational risk management context.

Risk management: two phases

Risk management is the process that allows managers to balance the operational and economic costs of protective measures and achieve gains in mission capability by protecting the IT systems and data that support their organisation's missions.[14]

Organisations develop and implement risk management strategies in order to reduce negative impacts and to provide a structured, consistent basis for making decisions around risk mitigation options. Risk management has two phases: risk assessment and risk treatment.

- Risk assessment is the process of identifying threats and assessing the likelihood of those threats exploiting some organisational vulnerability, as well as the potential impact of such an event occurring.

- Risk treatment is the process of responding to identified risks.

Risk assessment, also known as risk analysis, is the process by which risks are identified and assessed. The assessment process then stops. Any decisions and/or actions taken in

---

[13] ISO27001, clause 4.2.1 - b3.
[14] NIST SP 800-30, clause 2.1.

light of the risk assessment are taken outside the risk assessment process, and are part of the risk treatment plan which, together with the risk assessment process, is the other constituent of *risk management*. Risk management is the superset of, and therefore includes, risk assessment.

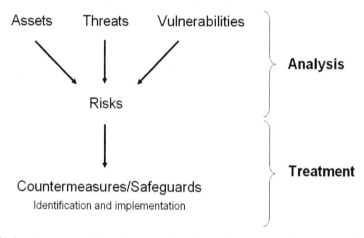

Risk assessment/analysis and risk treatment are the two sub-processes of risk management

Figure 1: Risk management

While it is true to say that the risk management process starts with a risk assessment, it is helpful to have a broader understanding of the overall environment in which most risk management activity takes place.

Risk management, as we have said, includes both risk assessment (or analysis) and risk treatment, and is a discipline that exists to deal with *non-speculative* risks, those risks from which *only* a loss can occur. In other words, *speculative* risks, those from which *either* a profit *or* a loss can occur, are the subject of the organisation's business strategy, whereas non-speculative risks, those risks which can reduce the value of the assets with which the organisation undertakes its speculative activity, are (usually) the subject of a risk management plan (in ISO27001, a 'risk treatment plan'). These non-speculative risks are sometimes called permanent or 'pure' risks, in order to differentiate them from the crisis and speculative types.

Risk management plans usually have four, linked, objectives. These are to:

- eliminate risks;

- reduce those that can't be eliminated to 'acceptable' levels; and then to either:

  - live with them, exercising carefully the controls that keep them 'acceptable'; or
  - transfer them, by means of insurance, to some other organisation.

The following diagram illustrates the concept of 'controlling' risk. One only pays attention to those risks which have a likelihood of occurring and will have a negative impact. The greater the likelihood, or the more negative the impact, the greater the risk.

Controls, or risk mitigation, should be designed to reduce likelihood and/or impact such that the magnitude of the risk is reduced below a tolerance threshold. This tolerance threshold is also often known as the risk acceptance level.

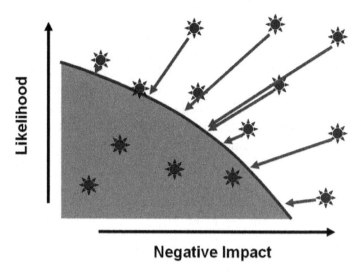

Negative Impact

Risk treatment plans reduce identified risks to the agreed risk acceptance level, here represented by the shaded area.

Figure 2: Risk treatment

Pure, permanent risks are usually identifiable in economic terms; they have a financially measurable potential impact upon the assets of the organisation. Risk management strategies are usually, therefore, based on an assessment of the economic benefits that the organisation can derive from an investment in a particular control or combination of controls. In other words, for every control that the organisation might implement, the calculation would be that the cost of implementation would be outweighed, preferably significantly, by the economic benefits that derive from, or economic losses that are avoided as a result of, its implementation.

The organisation should define its criteria for accepting risks (for example, it might say that it will accept any risk whose economic impact is less than the cost of controlling it) and for controlling risks (for example, it might say that any risk that has both a high likelihood and a high impact must be controlled to an identified level, or threshold). The enterprise risk management framework is, most usually, the framework within which organisations define their risk acceptance criteria in the light of their risk appetite and, as a result of which, define their systems of internal control.

Enterprise risk management

Enterprise risk management (ERM) is an increasingly important component of corporate governance and it provides an overall context for internal control activities.

Turnbull Guidance

The Turnbull Guidance[15], within the UK's Combined Code on Corporate Governance, is very clear on the steps that UK-listed companies should take in respect of risk: paragraph 19 of the Turnbull Guidance states that:

An internal control system encompasses the policies, processes, tasks, behaviours and other aspects of a company that, taken together:

- Facilitate its effective and efficient operation by enabling it to respond appropriately to significant business, operational, financial, compliance and other risks to achieving the company's objectives. This includes the safeguarding of assets from inappropriate use or from loss or fraud and ensuring that liabilities are identified and managed;

---

[15] Revised Turnbull Guidance published October 2005, available for download from *http://www.frc.org.uk/corporate/internalcontrol.cfm* .

- Help ensure the quality of internal and external reporting. This requires the maintenance of proper records and processes that generate a flow of timely, relevant and reliable information from within and outside the organisation;

- Help ensure compliance with applicable laws and regulations, and also with internal policies with respect to the conduct of business.

Paragraph 20 recognises that 'a company's system of internal control ... will include ... information and communications processes'. Paragraph 12 is clear that 'internal controls ... should include all types of controls including those of an operational and compliance nature, as well as internal financial controls'.

Basel 2

Pillar 1 of the Basel 2 Accord aims to align a bank's minimum capital requirements more closely to its actual risk of economic loss, aiming to establish an explicit capital charge for a 'bank's exposures to the risk of losses caused by failures in systems, processes, or staff or that are caused by external events'.[16] Those banks whose approaches to measuring, managing and controlling their operational risk exposures are appropriate to the risk area will have lower capital requirements.

---

[16] BIS Press Release, 26 June 2004.

COSO

A widely respected ERM framework is the one developed by COSO,[17] the body that was also responsible for developing the internal control framework that has been used in the vast majority of organisations to demonstrate compliance with the Sarbanes-Oxley Act of 2002 (SOX). The COSO *ERM – Integrated Framework* is in line with both Turnbull and Basel 2 when it defines ERM as:

... a process, effected by an entity's board of directors, management and other personnel, applied in strategy setting and across the enterprise, designed to identify potential events that may affect the entity, and manage risks to be within its risk appetite, to provide reasonable assurance regarding the achievement of entity objectives.

This definition contains many of the attributes that are also relevant to information security risk management. ERM objectives include:

- aligning risk appetite and strategy;
- consistently applying risk treatment criteria (enhancing risk response decisions), with the options to: accept, reject, transfer, control;
- reducing operational surprises and losses;
- identifying and managing multiple and cross-enterprise risks;
- seizing opportunities – after considering a full range of potential events;
- enabling risk-related deployment of capital.

---

[17] The Committee of Sponsoring Organizations of the Treadway Commission (www.coso.org).

Organisations that already have an ERM framework of some description in place are at an advantage in taking forward the ISO27001 risk management process, which should be slotted seamlessly within that overarching corporate ERM framework. The ERM objectives and risk acceptance criteria should be carried through into the ISO27001 risk management process, which should contribute to providing the board and management with a greater depth and breadth of assurance that information risk is being managed within pre-approved guidelines.

A pre-existing ERM is not, though, a pre-requisite for the successful development and implementation of an ISO27001 ISMS. Organisations that do not already have in place such a framework will need, at the very least, to develop their approach to risk sufficiently to be able to ensure that their information security risk assessment is business-driven, and is structured, systematic and reproducible. Moreover, the risk assessment approach will have to take into account the organisation's 'business and legal or regulatory requirements, and contractual security obligations'[18].

It is also not necessary to wait until the organisation develops a strategic approach to risk, or even an ERM framework. Information security management needs to be tackled more urgently than the timeframe that the development of an ERM framework will usually allow.

There are always issues of integration that have to be addressed when an ISO27001 risk assessment methodology is being developed within or alongside a broader, more

---

[18] ISO27001, clause 4.2.1 - b2.

strategic approach to risk management. For instance, definitions, roles and responsibilities could all be different, timeframes could be seriously out of alignment, and the ERM framework quite often tackles risk on a top-down basis, while ISO27001 requires a bottom-up approach to the identification and control of risk.

CHAPTER 2: RISK ASSESSMENT METHODOLOGIES

In this book we use the terms 'method' and 'methodology' interchangeably. A method is (as most standard dictionaries explain) simply a 'way of doing something'. A method, in other words, will contain principles and procedures, describing both what must be done and how it must be done. A risk assessment methodology, therefore, is a description of the principles and procedures (preferably documented) that describe how information security risks should be assessed and evaluated.

An effective, defined, ISO27001 information security risk assessment methodology should meet the requirements of ISO27001 and, in doing so, should provide the organisation (particularly its board and management) with an assurance that all the relevant risks have been factored into the process, and that there is a commonly defined and understood means of communicating and acting on the results of that risk assessment. This does, of course, also mean that there will be a wider and better understanding, across the organisation, of the risks that are being dealt with, and of the practical business support budget that will be required in order to implement the required controls.

We recognise that there are many established risk assessment methodologies. However, as we said earlier, an ISO27001 risk assessment has to contain, as a minimum, a specific set of steps and many currently recognised methodologies simply do not meet the requirements of ISO27001. This is because they do not contain the required steps, or because they do not address organisational risk, or

2: Risk Assessment Methodologies

even because they provide a primarily technology-focused information security risk assessment. We are not going to address those methodologies here.

Publicly available risk assessment standards

There are three standards that exist around ISO27001, and these are particularly useful and pertinent to the development of an ISO27001 risk assessment methodology. The key standards that we refer to here are:

- ISO27002

- ISO27005.

- In the UK, BS7799-3:2006[19] (*Information Security Management Systems – Part 3: Guidelines for information security risk management*) is also available as guidance on the subject. As this book has an international audience, we will draw primarily on ISO27005, and will take additional input from BS7799-3:2006 where appropriate.

NIST SP 800-30 (*Risk Management Guide for Information Technology Systems*) was published in July 2002 and is still current. Like ISO27005 and BS7799-3, it is a code of practice, not a specification. It provides guidance that is consistent with the requirements of ISO27001 and we have, therefore, drawn on the NIST document wherever it provides additional, useful guidance.

---

[19] In the UK, ISO/IEC 27001 is dual-numbered as BS7799-2, ISO/IEC 27002 is dual-numbered as BS7799-1 (they are exactly the same standards, with alternative names) and BS7799-3 fits neatly into that numbering sequence. BS7799-3, however, is not the same standard as ISO/IEC 27005.

ISO27002, the international code of information security best practice, identifies three sources for establishing an organisation's information security requirements: the risks that the organisation faces; the risks arising from the compliance and contractual requirements imposed on the organisation in each of the jurisdictions in which it operates; and the 'particular set of principles, objectives and business requirements for information processing that an organization has developed to support its operations', which should largely fall out of the IT architecture the organisation has established.

Clause 4.2.1 - c of ISO27001 (Define a systematic approach to risk assessment) says an appropriate risk assessment, suited to the ISMS, and to the identified business, legal and regulatory requirements, *shall* be undertaken. The steps in the risk assessment process are, as we shall see, to identify: the information assets (i.e. anything that has value to the organisation) within the scope of the ISMS, owners for those assets, the threats to the assets, the vulnerabilities that might be exploited by those threats and the impacts that losses of confidentiality, integrity and availability may have on the assets, hence determining the degree of risk. While the risk assessment steps are mandatory, we still have to define a methodology for assessing risk and, for help in that, we will turn again to ISO27002 and ISO27005.

ISO27002 provides substantial guidance on risk assessment, but no detailed guidance on how the assessment is to be conducted, because every organisation is encouraged to choose that approach which is most applicable for its industry, complexity and risk environment. In its introduction, ISO27002 describes risk assessment in terms compatible with our introduction to it and also refers the reader looking for more guidance to

ISO13335-3, which contains examples of risk assessment methodologies. ISO13335-3 has been withdrawn and replaced by ISO27005.

ISO27005 (Annex E) identifies only two possible approaches to risk assessment. These are:

- carry out an initial high-level assessment of the information assets to identify and prioritise treatment of those assets that have the most exposure, and implementing controls that relate to the most critical risks;

- conduct a detailed, formal risk assessment, using a formal methodology.

Either of these approaches would work for an ISO27001 ISMS; the critical thing is to think through the strategic implications of starting with a high-level risk assessment and identify how and when you move, in due course, to a detailed exercise.

ISO27001 and ISO27002 variously adopt (from ISO Guide 73:2002) definitions of risk, risk analysis, risk assessment, risk evaluation, risk management and risk treatment. We recommend that these definitions are, for the sake of consistency, adopted by any organisation tackling risk management and, as indicated at the outset, this book will proceed on that basis.

BS7799-3:2006 is another guidance document that describes different approaches to an information security risk assessment, and this could also be consulted when determining the methodology for an organisation.

ISO27002 is clear, in its introduction, that risk assessment is a 'systematic study of assets, threats, vulnerabilities and impacts to assess the probability and consequences of risks' or, in our terms, the systematic and methodical consideration of:

a) the business harm likely to result from a range of business failures; and

b) the realistic likelihood of such failures occurring.

The inclusion of this issue in ISO27002 clause 4, dealing with risk assessments, indicates its importance and the expectation that every control decision that an organisation makes will explicitly reflect a risk assessment. This clause was not in previous editions of the standard.

The risk assessment must be a formal process. In other words, the process must be planned and the input data, its analysis and the results should all be recorded. 'Formal' does not mean that risk assessment tools must be used, although, in most situations, they will improve the process and add significant value; in many organisations, it will not in fact be possible to carry out a risk assessment without using an appropriate tool. (We provide information on risk assessment tools later in this book.) The complexity of the risk assessment will depend on the complexity of the organisation and of the risks under review, and in particular, the approach to grouping assets. The techniques employed to carry it out should be consistent with this complexity and the level of assurance required by the board.

Risk is a function of likelihood and impact. The risk equation, to which we will return again and again, is:

Risk = Likelihood x Impact

This equation can be expanded to recognise that vulnerabilities are the exposure or weakness that a threat can exploit to compromise an asset and that, by 'likelihood', we simply mean the likelihood of the threat exploiting the vulnerability; and, adopting the principle that the impact value is the full consequence of an asset being compromised (as will be discussed in Chapter 10) we can restate the equation thus:

Risk = (probability of threat exploiting vulnerability) x (total impact cost of asset being exploited)

Our risk assessment methodology needs to equip us to ascribe values to these factors in the risk equation. While there are many different approaches, they essentially break down into two: qualitative and quantitative.

Qualitative *versus* quantitative

In conducting the impact analysis, consideration should be given to the advantages and disadvantages of quantitative *versus* qualitative assessments. A quantitative methodology is one that uses (primarily) quantitative input, i.e. mathematical data, and a qualitative one uses primarily non-mathematical input.

The main advantage of the qualitative impact analysis is that it prioritises the risks and identifies areas for immediate improvement in addressing the vulnerabilities. The disadvantage of the qualitative analysis is that it does not provide specific quantifiable measurements of the magnitude of the impacts, thus making a cost-benefit analysis of any recommended controls difficult to calculate precisely.

The major advantage of a quantitative impact analysis is, therefore, that it provides a measurement of the magnitude of some (but not all) impacts which can be used in the cost-benefit analysis of recommended controls. We say 'but not all' because there are some impacts (loss of reputation, loss of credibility, loss of public confidence, etc.) that are extremely difficult, if not impossible, to quantify meaningfully. At best, one may only be able to apply qualitative measures, such as 'high' or 'very high', without even being able to quantify the meaning of the term.

The further disadvantage of quantitative methodologies is that, depending on the numerical ranges used to describe the impacts, the meaning of the quantitative impact analysis may be unclear, as a result of which the result would have to be interpreted in a qualitative manner.

Quantitative risk analysis

This approach looks at two figures: one for the probability of an event occurring and the other the likely loss should it occur. A single figure is produced from these two elements, by simply multiplying the potential loss (measured in monetary terms) by its probability (measured as a percentage or fraction of times per year, say). This is sometimes called the annual loss expectancy (ALE) or the estimated annual cost (EAC). Clearly, the higher the number that an event or risk has, the more serious it is for the organisation. It is then possible to rank risks in order of magnitude (ALE) and to make decisions based upon this.

The problem with this type of risk analysis is that so long can be taken in producing a figure, and then revisiting the figures in light of comparison with other assets, threats and vulnerabilities, that no progress toward actual implementation of the ISMS is made. In some cases, this approach can promote or reflect complacency about the real significance of particular risks. The monetary value of the potential loss is also often subjectively assessed (i.e. it uses qualitative data) and, when the two components are multiplied together, the answer is equally subjective. A methodology which produces results that are largely dependent on subjective individual decisions, which are unlikely to be similar to the decisions of another person, is not one which will produce results that are reproducible and comparable and it will, therefore, fail the requirements of ISO27001.

In addition, controls and countermeasures often have to tackle a number of potential events and the events themselves are frequently interrelated. A detailed ranking in order of ALE can make it difficult to identify these interrelationships and can lead to poor decisions about controls; this approach is not, therefore, recommended.

Nevertheless, we recognise that a number of organisations have successfully adopted quantitative risk analysis.

Qualitative risk analysis – the ISO27001 approach

ISO27002 provides guidance that the risk assessment methodology should enable the organisation to 'estimate' the magnitude of security risks and use this information to make decisions about 'proportionate' security controls. 'Estimation' and 'proportionate' are two principles that form the basis of a qualitative risk assessment methodology, one that doesn't need a precisely calculated ALE. A qualitative methodology ranks identified risks in relation to one another, using a qualitative or hierarchical scale (such as: very serious – serious – bearable – not a problem). It is, therefore, based on similar qualitative hierarchies, or scales, of threat and vulnerability seriousness, and of likelihood and impact.

One of the key concepts for risk assessment is contained in the BS7799-3 guidance that says that assets should be valued to take 'account of the identified legal and business requirements and the impacts resulting from a loss of confidentiality, integrity and availability' (clause 5.1). It also says that 'one way to express asset values is to use the business impacts that unwanted incidents, such as disclosure, modification, non-availability and/or destruction, would have to the asset and the related business interests that would be directly or indirectly damaged' (clause 5.4).

Finally, states BS7799-3, impact 'values should be identified that express the potential business impacts if the confidentiality, integrity or availability, or any other important property of the asset is damaged' (clause 5.4). It suggests that a standard asset valuation scale should be defined for assets to assist asset owners in correctly valuing their assets.

ISO27005 is less clear on this subject; it talks (as 8.2.1.6) about 'identification of consequences'; it defines a consequence as 'loss of effectiveness, adverse operating conditions, loss of business, reputation, damage, etc.' and says that, in the risk assessment process, the 'consequences that losses of confidentiality, integrity and availability may have on the assets should be identified.' Impact and consequences are really different words for much the same concept, which is to establish the level of damage the organisation will suffer as a result of any given security breach?

A qualitative methodology is by far the most widely used approach to risk analysis and it meets the requirements of clause 4.2.1 - d (Identify the risks) of ISO27001. The risk level is based on banding values or levels for likelihood and impact, so that exact calculations are not required. ISO27005 says that a qualitative methodology 'uses a scale of qualifying attributes to describe the magnitude of potential consequences (e.g. low, medium, high).'[20] However, in order to ensure that the results are comparable and reproducible, the bands must be defined so that a medium impact in the judgement of one person can be demonstrated as comparable to a medium impact in another's. The output of the risk equation would then also be qualitative.

A five-level risk scale, for instance, might lead to risks being placed on a scale that identifies them as:

Risk level	**Risk treatment action required**
Very high	Unacceptable: action needs to be taken immediately.
High	Unacceptable: action to be taken as soon as possible.
Medium	Action required and to be taken within a reasonable timescale.
Low	Acceptable: no action required as a result of risk assessment. Any action should be the subject of a full cost-benefit analysis.
Very low:	Acceptable: no action required.

---

[20] ISO27005 – 8.2.2.1

The output of the risk equation can be represented using a scale, such as the three-level likelihood and impact version below (which produces a five-level risk scale), and which relates the identified impact of an event occurring to an assessed likelihood of it actually happening.

Likelihood				
	High	Medium risk	High risk	Very high risk
	Medium	Low risk	Medium risk	High risk
	Low	Very low risk	Low risk	Medium risk
		Low	Medium	High
		Impact		

Figure 3: Three-level risk matrix

The methodology recommended by this book, and developed fully in Chapter 7, is a qualitative one. Working methods for assessing impact, likelihood, threat and vulnerability are all important to the qualitative methodology, and the balance of this chapter will review the key concepts for each of these before we turn, in the next chapter, to their application in an ISO27001 risk assessment.

One of the key, practical benefits of a qualitative risk assessment methodology is that it recognises that there is inevitably a subjective aspect to any risk assessment exercise, and it provides a framework in which such assessments can give comparable and reproducible results. It also allows you to complete the initial risk assessment within a reasonable time period, and accepts that, in assessing and controlling risk, it is preferable to be 'approximately correct, rather than precisely wrong'.

Other risk assessment methodologies

CRAMM

The CCTA[21] Risk Analysis and Management Method (CRAMM) originated in 1985. Release version 5.1 became available in 2005. It follows three stages:

- asset identification and valuation;
- threat and vulnerability assessment;
- countermeasure selection and recommendation.

It applies a qualitative risk assessment methodology at an individual asset level, and it values assets primarily in relation to the impact that would be experienced by a breach in confidentiality, integrity and availability. The CRAMM methodology is in line with the requirements of ISO27001, although the methodology now is primarily implemented through the use of CRAMM tools. There is a description of the CRAMM tools in Chapter 5.

OCTAVE

One well-known approach that *can* be tailored to meet the requirements of ISO27001 is OCTAVE and the approach

---

[21] Central Computer and Telecommunications Agency, a UK Government Agency.

provides useful input for any organisation developing its own practical approach. Note, though, that OCTAVE does not, on its own, meet the requirements of ISO27001.

The Operationally Critical Threat, Asset, and Vulnerability Evaluation set of criteria, or OCTAVE[22], was developed by Carnegie Mellon University. It is a set of criteria that can be developed into many different methodologies, and can use either quantitative or qualitative approaches; as long as those methodologies adhere to the OCTAVE criteria, each is recognised as an OCTAVE-consistent method.

The OCTAVE criteria consist of a set of principles, attributes and outputs. These include the principle of self-direction (i.e. the risk assessment is resourced from within the organisation being assessed), using a multi-disciplinary team (an attribute), and that outputs will relate to three phases of assessment.

To apply OCTAVE, a small team from across the organisation works together to consider the security needs of the organisation whilst balancing operational risk, security practices and technology. This team is known as the Analysis Team.

OCTAVE factors all aspects of risk into decision-making. That is to say, it considers assets, threats, vulnerabilities and organisational impact and includes them in the process. OCTAVE requires the Analysis Team to follow a specific series of steps:

- identify information-related assets that are important to the organisation;

---

[22] See www.cert.org/octave/methodintro.html

- focus risk analysis activities on those assets judged to be most critical;
- consider the relationships among critical assets, the threats to those assets, and vulnerabilities that can be exploited by the threats;
- evaluate risks in an operational context – considering how assets are used in the business and how those assets are at risk due to security threats; and
- create a practical protection strategy for organisational improvement as well as risk mitigation plans to reduce the risk to the organisation's critical assets.

OCTAVE uses a three-phased approach to enable the Analysis Team to produce a comprehensive picture of the organisation's information security needs:

- **Phase 1: Build asset-based threat profiles** – the Analysis Team determines which information-related assets are important to the organisation and identifies the arrangements (controls) that are currently in place to protect those assets. They identify the assets that are most important to the organisation and describe the security requirements for each critical asset. They then identify threats to each of these assets, creating a threat profile for that asset. ISO27001, in contrast, requires the involvement of individual asset owners, and expects that all assets – not simply the most critical – will be included.

- **Phase 2: Identify infrastructure vulnerabilities** – the Analysis Team examines network access paths, identifying classes of information technology components related to each critical asset, and then determines the extent to which each class of component is resistant to network attacks. ISO27001, by comparison, looks for all potential vulnerabilities, including physical ones, to be identified.

- **Phase 3: Develop security strategy and plans** – the Analysis Team identifies risks to the identified critical assets and decides what to do about them, creating mitigation plans to address the risks to the assets, based on the Phase 1 and 2 analyses.

Carnegie Mellon University has developed three methodologies using the OCTAVE criteria: the original Octave Method (which forms the basis of the Octave Body of Knowledge), for large and complex organisations or those which are split across a number of geographical locations; Octave-S for small organisations with between 20 and 80 people and which are not complex in structure; and Octave-Allegro, a more streamlined approach for information security assessment and assurance.

IRAM, SARA, SPRINT and FIRM

The Information Security Forum (ISF) is a private, members-only organisation with some 260 members worldwide. It has developed a set of methodologies and tools which are available only to its members; these include tools for carrying out information security risk assessments. These tools, which are not publicly available, are designed to be used complementarily, and are:

- IRAM: Information Risk Analysis Methodologies;

- SARA: Simple to Apply Risk Analysis, primarily aimed at risk in business-critical systems;

- SPRINT: Simplified Process for Risk Identification, primarily aimed at important – but not critical – systems;
- FIRM: Fundamental Information Risk Management.

The ISF toolset supports all the fundamental risk management phases, and has many components that can be useful in an ISO27001 risk assessment. However, its focus is on business systems, not on individual assets, and therefore, the ISF tools would need to be adapted for use in the ISO27001, asset-based risk assessment environment.

As they are not publicly available tools (they are only available for use by members of the ISF – about 260 large, global organisations), and therefore, not likely to be of use to the majority of organisations tackling information security risk assessments, we have not developed them further here.

Other methodologies

DRAM, the Delphi Risk Assessment Method, and FRAP, the Facilitated Risk Assessment Process, are another two risk assessment methodologies. There are many others. The ENISA lists some of the less widely-used methodologies: *http://rm-inv.enisa.europa.eu/rm_ra_methods.html* .

The purpose of this book is to provide you with the basis for a methodology that you can use to carry out a specific ISO27001-compliant risk assessment. There is, therefore, little value in an extensive survey and comparison of different methodologies.

CHAPTER 3: RISK MANAGEMENT OBJECTIVES

We identified, in Chapter 1, the probability that most organisations already have in place a range of risk assessment approaches, driven perhaps by regulation as much as by the board's desire to meet its fiduciary duties to shareholders and other stakeholders in the organisation.

Risk acceptance or tolerance

An organisation's risk acceptance criteria (which we discussed in Chapter 1) are defined in its overall approach to risk management and are contained in its information security policy.

ISO27001 says that the ISMS policy must 'align with the organization's strategic risk management context' (clause 4.2.1 - b3) or its ERM framework, if it already has one in place. What this means is that the organisation, in order to focus effectively on managing risk, should not have a number of different levels of risk tolerance, or risk acceptance. When an organisation approaches risk management on a piecemeal basis, with different individuals or departments leading different risk management efforts without any common direction or guidance, it can easily find itself in a situation where it has, by default, a number of different levels of risk acceptance. These are illustrated in the example overleaf:

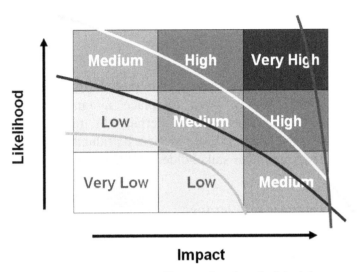

Organisations that have different levels of risk tolerance for different aspects of their operations (e.g. information security; health and safety; financial control; operational risk) find it difficult to provide coherent management.

Figure 4: Inconsistent risk tolerance

Not all these different levels of risk acceptance, or of risk tolerance, are necessarily acceptable to the board. Organisations should, rather, set risk tolerance levels that are consistently applied through all their operations, irrespective of whether they are IT, financial or operational in nature. The ISO27001 requirement that the risk assessment methodology should take the organisational context into account is designed exactly to ensure this level of coordination.

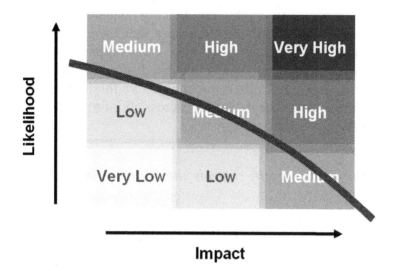

Figure 5: Risk tolerance or acceptance: criteria applied consistently across all activities

Information security risk management objectives

NIST's SP 800-30, *Risk Management Guide for Information Technology Systems*, is consistent with the ERM frameworks we have been discussing and is also reflected, as we shall see, in ISO27001. It defines the risk management objectives as follows:

To enable the organisation to accomplish its missions(s) by:

(1) better securing (safeguarding the confidentiality, integrity and availability of) the organization's information;

(2) enabling management to take well-informed risk management decisions to justify information security related expenditure; and

(3) assisting management in controlling risks and exercising good stewardship.

In essence, one might say that an organisation's risk management objective is to ensure that there is a proper balance of safeguards against the risks of failing to meet business objectives: neither too much nor too little[23]. By extension, the risk management objective for an ISMS is to limit risk to an acceptable level across all information assets for all information security risks.

Information security controls and return on investment (ROI)

In all too many organisations, the information security controls historically adopted were selected on the basis of informed opinion, rather than as a result of a systematic and reproducible business-oriented risk assessment. There is, in fact, a direct relationship between the level of investment and the return on that investment: those organisations that under-invest in information security have as negative a return on their investment as do those organisations that over-invest in it.

Optimum ROI in information security control investment is driven by selecting and implementing those controls which will mitigate specific, identified risks to specific, identified assets, and whose total cost of implementation is lower than the potential cost of impact of the identified risk. Above all, those controls whose design is predicated on a proper understanding of the required balance between the confidentiality, integrity and availability (particularly to business users) of information are the most cost-effective and useful of controls.

---

[23] This is sometimes known as the 'Goldilocks Solution'.

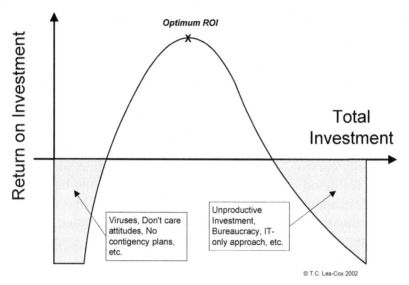

© T.C. Lea-Cox 2002

**Figure 6: Return on investment in information
security controls**

The above graph indicates clearly that too much investment
in information security controls can be as bad as too little.
However:

- simply removing existing information security controls,
  or safeguards, in order to improve the availability of
  information to business users may increase the risk of
  loss to unacceptable levels;

- having too many safeguards in place – a not infrequent
  characteristic of organisations where the board has
  abdicated its responsibility for information security
  control decisions to the IT department – quite often
  makes the information security system too expensive or
  bureaucratic, not just in respect of the direct cost of
  implementation but also in relation to the negative

impact the safeguards have on business productivity; and, finally,

- risk assessment can be used as a method by which expenditure on security and contingency-planning can be justified.

The practical approach, for organisations who wish to maximise the return on their investment in information security controls, is to select controls, having first analysed the likelihood of a compromise occurring, on the basis of their economic value to the organisation. This means selecting controls with specific reference to the value – and the potential impact on the business of losing – specific information assets.

High value assets – faced with high risks – should be protected by more extensive controls than low value ones. The information security risk assessment must, therefore, be carried out at individual asset level, and controls should only be selected and applied to those assets where management has determined that the potential loss to the organisation is such that investment in controls is appropriate.

This is an obviously sensible approach: it ensures that limited financial and human resources are prioritised and allocated to counter the biggest risks to the organisation, rather than applied indiscriminately across all assets of the organisation. An information security risk assessment quite often enables organisations to identify areas in which their controls are in excess of their real requirements and it, therefore, enables resources to be freed-up for re-investment in more critical areas.

In principle, therefore, the risk assessment must be conducted at a detailed, individual asset level. By 'individual asset level', we mean individual laptops, servers, databases, folders, e-mails, records and so on. Typically, however, organisations attempt to simplify the risk assessment process by aggregating information assets and then identifying generic threats to that aggregation. This over-simplification usually leads to dissimilar assets being treated in the same manner, typically as if they all had the attributes of the most valuable, and/or most vulnerable, within the group and, as a result, the controls that are selected are not actually required for a number of items within the group.

Risk management and PDCA

ISO27001 is very clear about the risk management approach that it requires and where risk management sits in the project plan.

ISO27001 adopts the Plan-Do-Check-Act (PDCA) model that anyone familiar with other management system standards and various change tools will recognise. That is to say that, to implement an ISO27001-compliant ISMS, an organisation needs to 'plan' what it is going to do, carry out those plans, i.e. 'do' it, 'check' that what they have done has achieved the desired objective, and then 'act' on any shortfall.

The ISO27001 specification puts the following tasks in each of the PDCA stages:

- Plan (establish the ISMS): establish the scope, security policy, targets, processes and procedures relevant to assessing risk and carry out risk assessment in order to improve information security so that it delivers results in accordance with the organisation's overall policies and objectives.

- Do (implement and operate the ISMS): implement and operate the security policy, and the controls that were chosen as a result of the risk assessment process, as well as the processes and procedures of the ISMS.

- Check (monitor and review the ISMS): assess and, where applicable, measure process performance against security policy, objectives and practical experience and report the results to management for review. This will include measuring the effectiveness of the management system and the controls that it implements.

- Act (maintain and improve the ISMS): take corrective and preventive actions, based on the results of the management review, to achieve continual improvement of the ISMS.

Once the 'act' stage is completed the organisation then starts over again, planning what to do to improve the ISMS. It is, therefore, correct to say that an organisation which has embarked on an ISO27001 project is in a PDCA continuum, and that the aim of this cyclic experience is to identify and manage risks, and drive continual improvement to the ISMS.

Risk assessment, in other words, initially takes place during the planning stage of the ISO27001 ISMS project. Control selection and implementation cannot start until after the risk assessment process is completed. Put another way, the risk assessment informs the management of risk and is thus critical to the creation of the risk treatment plan. The relationship between risk assessment and risk treatment, and their position on the PDCA continuum, is clear and is as shown in the diagram below:

Figure 7: Risk management and the PDCA cycle

More accurately, we should say that risk assessment always falls totally within the 'plan' stage of the ISMS project cycle, and that some of the risk management, in fact the majority of the decision-making around control objectives and controls, is also within this stage, as that is what informs the risk treatment plan and the organisation's Statement of Applicability.[24] These, in turn, inform further the operational structure and content of the ISMS, which implements and manages the controls that bring the identified risks within an acceptable level.

---

[24] See ISO27001 clause 4.2.1 and Chapter 10.

Table 1 of ISO27005 identifies how the PDCA cycle is aligned with the information security risk management process:

Plan	Establish the context
	Risk assessment
	Develop risk treatment plan
	Risk acceptance
Do	Implementation of risk treatment plan
Check	Continual monitoring and reviewing of risks
Act	maintain and improve the information security risk management process

The risk assessment, of course, also provides the organisation with a baseline for improvement. The extent to which this baseline is useful depends on whether you have conducted the risk assessment in light of the controls that are already in place, or on the basis that no controls are applied. Both approaches have benefits, and we will return to their pros and cons later.

Risk assessment is, in conclusion, the key activity required during the planning stage of the ISMS project. Every single control that is to be implemented will be selected on the basis of the risk assessment, and the risk assessment must be completed before any controls are implemented. Risk assessment is also an ongoing activity of the ISMS; whenever there is a change in the risk environment, or of business requirements, or to the asset – indeed, whenever there is any change that might affect the risk profile of the asset – a new risk assessment will be required.

In fact, risk assessment is so central to information security management that we see it as the *core competence* of the ISMS.

PDCA and the risk acceptance criteria

Whilst ISO27001 expects the board to finalise its risk acceptance criteria and risk assessment methodology before the risk acceptance process itself is started, experience teaches that most organisations need to apply the PDCA principle to this aspect of their ISMS as well.

In other words, senior management and the board should determine, initially, what the acceptance criteria and methodology should be. It is not unusual for either excessive caution or unexpected bravado to underpin this initial phase of development work – not least because the total value or full nature of the organisation's information assets is not always fully appreciated at this early stage.

The initial methodology and risk acceptance criteria should then be applied in a test environment (the 'do' phase of the risk acceptance criteria PDCA process), with a reasonably wide range of information assets. These tests will lead to potential risk treatment decisions which management and the board can assess (the 'check' phase) for reasonableness and acceptability in light of the broader risk management and investment context. The methodology and criteria can then be revised to produce results that are more acceptable to management and this then becomes the 'release' version.

It is worth retaining this perspective throughout the risk assessment process, so that, if results are generated which seem out of line with common sense, the risk assessor can revert to the risk assessment criteria and methodology and, if necessary, propose improvements to it. Of course, improvements – and the reasons for them – should be documented and will form part of the ISMS documentation.

CHAPTER 4: ROLES AND RESPONSIBILITIES

Risk management is a process that involves people and, while many of the people involved in this process will already have specific responsibilities inside the organisation, it is important to identify precisely the contribution they are expected to make to the risk management process.

ISO27005 recommends (clause 7.4) that 'the organization and responsibilities for the information security risk management process should be set up and maintained' and, in a footnote, comments that the creation of an organisation capable of carrying out a risk assessment could be regarded as 'one of the resources required by ISO/IEC 27001.'

Senior management commitment

Without senior level management commitment it is unlikely an ISO27001 project would get as far as a risk assessment, but if it did, it certainly would not get much further.

In our experience, the risk assessment stage of the project is one of the most testing. The sheer amount of time and effort required to undertake a risk assessment that is sufficiently detailed to meet the requirements of ISO27001 is always underestimated at the start of the project, and this is when the drive and clout of senior management commitment is essential. That is, of course, assuming the senior managers understood what they were committing to in the first place!

One of the first things the project team should stage, in any ISMS project, is a board briefing which ensures that the senior managers who are signing up to the project, and committing the resources and effort to achieve the objective of certification (or at least an ISO27001-conforming ISMS), do so from an adequately informed position.

Of course, this means that they need to be aware of the costs and amount of work required, but also the benefits that follow, including the indirect benefits of, for example, identifying and protecting specific information assets and of changing and improving the mindset of those managers responsible for them. In some organisations just producing an information asset register is a major undertaking and can warrant a considerable project in its own right, delivering benefits when the invoices and 'Friday cake club' schedule are suitably segregated and asset 'owners' identified.

As this book explains, the risk assessment process will involve a number of staff for a considerable amount of time. When done correctly, management and senior staff will be involved and their time will suddenly become all the more precious. When senior management make an adequately informed commitment to the project, sufficient encouragement and resources should be made available for the project to progress to plan and to time.

Another benefit and product of senior management commitment should be the assignment of a dedicated resource for coordinating risk management policies and tasks. Assigning a central risk management coordination resource (which we discuss further, below) is a critical success factor. The intention is that this central focal point carries out coordination activities, acts as a route for risk issues to be brought to the attention of senior management, ensures suitable tools and resources are available, and provides guidance and advice to all those elsewhere in the business who are actually carrying out the risk assessment activities.

Not only does such a central resource ensure that risk management, initially, and then subsequently, receives the attention it deserves, but it also provides the essential structure in which risk assessment results throughout the organisation can be accurately described as 'repeatable and comparable'. 'Repeatable and comparable' is a key requirement of the risk assessment methodology, as defined in ISO27001.

The (lead) risk assessor

It is entirely up to the individual organisation to choose who is to undertake, or rather coordinate, the risk assessment, and how. There are two issues to consider before deciding who. The first is that the standard expects that periodic reviews of security risks and related controls will be carried out – taking account of new threats and vulnerabilities, assessing the impact of changes in the business, its goals or processes, technology and/or its external environment (such as legislation, regulation or society) and simply to confirm that controls remain effective and appropriate. Periodic review is a fundamental requirement of any risk assessment or risk management strategy.

The second issue is that it is an assumption of the standard (stated in the foreword) 'that the execution of its provisions is entrusted to appropriately qualified and experienced people'. It is essential that the risk assessment is managed by an appropriately qualified and experienced person. This is logical; the key step on which the entire ISMS will be built needs, itself, to be solid. The ISO27001 auditor will, therefore, want to see documentary evidence of the formal qualifications and experience of this person; at least that they have been reviewed and accepted by management.

A number of organisations will, as we have seen, already have a risk management function, staffed by people with training that enables them to carry out risk assessments. The role of the risk management team is, usually, to systematically identify, evaluate and control potential losses to the organisation that may result from things that haven't happened yet. The skills and methodology of this group may, or may not, also meet the requirements of ISO27001. Either way, there are potentially significant benefits for such an organisation if its information security risk assessments can be carried out by the same function that handles all risk assessments.

The benefits lie not just in cost effectiveness, but in the fact that such a risk management, or risk control resource, will have an existing and ongoing understanding of the business, its goals and environment, and an appreciation of all the risks faced by the business in the pursuit of its objectives. Equally, they should be able to assess how all the different risks, and the steps taken to counter them, are related and coordinated. This, of course, also helps address the requirement that the risk assessment is conducted in the wider business risk context.

Many organisations, however, do not already have an internal risk management function. There are two possible ways to tackle the issue of risk assessment. The first is to hire an external consultant (or firm of consultants) to do it. The second is to train someone internally to do it. The second is preferable in most cases, as the risk assessment 'shall be reviewed at appropriately defined intervals as required' and having the expertise in-house enables this to be undertaken cost-effectively. It also increases ownership of the process and the resulting ISMS.

In circumstances where the organisation has existing arrangements with external suppliers for risk assessment services, or is in the process of setting up a risk management function or capability (in the context of responding to the requirements of the increasing corporate governance and regulatory requirements, perhaps), then it should, from the outset, investigate ways in which its risk assessment processes could be integrated.

It is more difficult for a smaller business to retain specialist information security expertise in house than for a larger one; the internal risk assessment role needs to be maintained over time and the person concerned needs to continue being trained and involved in both information security and risk assessment issues, both inside and outside the organisation.

The disadvantage of hiring external risk assessors, apart from the cost, is that the organisation does not necessarily get continuity of involvement from individuals within a firm of assessors. The advantage of the external hire, apart from it being a variable cost, is that the external assessor should be up to date on relevant issues and should be wholly objective. A possible middle route is to contract on a multi-year basis, with an appropriately trained individual or consultancy firm to personally provide this service as and when it is required, working closely with identified internal staff. However the organisation chooses to acquire this resource, it is crucial that s/he is in place and able to be fully involved in the risk analysis and assessment process that this book describes.

Other roles and responsibilities

We have already said, categorically, that board and senior management support for the ISMS and, by extension, for the risk management process is critical. However, senior management support on its own will not be sufficient for the organisation to succeed: responsibilities need to be devolved to a number of people throughout the organisation. The risk assessment process will rely on input from a wide range of sources, and all those people who are most able to provide knowledgeable and informed input and decisions must contribute to the process.

The people who should support[25] and participate in the risk management process include:

Chief Information Officer (CIO): is responsible for the organisation's IT planning, budgeting and performance, including its information security components. Decisions made in these areas should be based on an effective risk management programme. Unless the CIO has substantial business experience and can communicate effectively and convincingly across the business-technology gulf that exists in most organisations, the CIO should not lead the ISO27001 project. Achieving ISO27001 is a business change project, not an IT project.

Senior executive management: are accountable to the board and have ultimate operational responsibility for

---

[25] NIST SP 800-30 provided most of the detailed role descriptions used here.

achieving the organisation's goals. They must be committed to the project and must, therefore, ensure that the necessary resources are effectively applied to develop the capabilities needed to accomplish those goals. They must also assess and incorporate the results of the initial and ongoing risk assessment activity into their decision-making process. An effective risk management programme that assesses and mitigates information-related risks requires the support and involvement of senior management – without whose active and committed involvement an ISO27001 project is, in any case, doomed to fail.

Business managers (who are also likely to be information asset 'owners'): are responsible for determining the criticality and sensitivity of business operations and, therefore, of the information assets on which those business operations depend. Business managers are best placed to assess the real asset value which, as we shall see shortly, will inform the impact side of the risk assessment equation.

Business and functional managers: those responsible for business operations and the procurement process; they must also take an active role in the risk management process. These managers are the individuals with the authority and responsibility for making the trade-off decisions essential to achieving business objectives. Their involvement in the risk management process helps deliver effective security for the information systems, helping the organisation achieve its objectives with minimal expenditure on resources.

Information security officers (ISOs), information security managers and computer security officers: are responsible for their organisation's information security activity, including the implementation of risk treatment decisions. ISOs should all be appropriately qualified;

appropriate qualifications are those (such as CISM, CISMP) that are focused on managing information security, rather than its technical implementation.[26] ISOs have a leading role to play in introducing an appropriate, structured methodology that helps identify, evaluate and minimise risks to the information assets and IT systems that support the organisational objectives. Critically, therefore, ISOs must have risk assessment competence and the organisation needs to have made adequate provision for risk assessment training.

ISOs can also act internally as key consultants in support of senior management to help ensure the success of the ISMS project.

IT security practitioners (including network, system, application and database administrators, computer specialists, security analysts and security consultants): are responsible for the proper implementation of control requirements in their IT systems. IT security practitioners should be appropriately skilled and trained, and should have relevant, current technical qualifications (e.g. CCNA, CCSA)[27] related to those technologies for which they are specifically responsible.

As changes occur in the existing IT system environment (e.g. expansion in network connectivity, changes to the existing infrastructure and organisational policies, or the introduction of new technologies), the IT security

---

[26] See *www.itgovernance.co.uk/page.infosec_qualifications* for all the key information security management qualifications and graduate/post graduate courses. Each qualification has different strengths and weaknesses; it is not unusual for individuals to accumulate more than one qualification.

[27] See *www.itgovernance.co.uk/page.infosec_qualifications* for a list of some of the key, current vendor technical qualifications.

practitioners must support or use the risk management process to identify and assess new potential risks and implement new security controls as needed to safeguard their IT systems.

Technical/functional personnel: are most able to form practical and realistic opinions on the likelihood of occurrence of the threat-vulnerability combinations that will be identified as compromising individual information assets. Technical personnel include all those with relevant technical or functional expertise, including the facilities management team for physical security issues, HR for personnel, IT for information technology, those with responsibilities for utilities and other aspects of the corporate infrastructure, the finance team, the audit team, etc.

System and information asset owners: are responsible for ensuring that proper controls are in place to protect the integrity, confidentiality and availability of the information systems and information assets (data) they own. Typically, the system and information owners are also responsible for changes to their information assets. Thus, they might have to approve and sign off changes to their information systems (e.g. system enhancements, major changes to the software and hardware). The system and information owners must, therefore, understand their role in the risk management process and fully support it.

The initial role of the individual asset owner in the risk assessment project is two-fold: first, s/he is responsible for estimating the value of the asset for which s/he is accountable, following the principles set out in Chapter 6, and applying the appropriate level of sensitivity classification; second, s/he is responsible for identifying all threat-vulnerability combinations that might relate to the asset. Any risk assessment tool that you use must be capable of allowing asset owners to provide this information, either through some form of information collection device or through online functionality.

Training team: this should include subject-matter experts and the champion users of the organisation's information systems, and these people have a key role to play. Use of the information systems and data according to an organisation's policies, guidelines, and specific procedures are critical to mitigating risk and protecting the organisation's resources. To minimise risk to the information systems, it is essential that system and application users be provided with security awareness training. Therefore, the information security trainers or security/subject matter professionals must understand the risk management process, so that they can develop appropriate training materials and incorporate risk assessment into training programmes that are effective for the end users. Much of this training can be delivered through online learning or other media that ensures consistent delivery of a clearly articulated training message.

CHAPTER 5: RISK ASSESSMENT SOFTWARE

There are software tools that have been designed to assist in risk assessment and, although their use is not mandatory in the standard, it is practically impossible to carry out and maintain a useful risk assessment for an organisation that has more than about four workstations without using such a tool. It is essential that the risk assessment be completed methodically, systematically and comprehensively. An appropriate software tool, designed with ISO27001 in mind and kept up to date in terms of changing information security issues, can be effective in this process.

This is because the risk assessment is a complex and data-rich process. For an organisation of any size, the only practical way to carry it out is to create a database that contains details of all the assets within the scope of the ISMS, and then to link, to each asset, the details of its (multiple) threats and (multiple) vulnerabilities, and their likelihood and resulting impacts, together with details of the asset ownership and its confidentiality classification.

The risk assessment process is made enormously simpler if one can also use ready-made databases of threats and vulnerabilities. The database should also contain details of the control decisions made as a result of the risk assessment, so that, at a glance, it is easy to see what controls are in place for each asset within the ISMS.

This database must be updated in the light of new risk assessments, which should take place whenever there are changes to the assets or to any aspect of the risk environment. The number of software tools available for this purpose is increasing. To one extent or another they automate the risk assessment process and generate the Statement of Applicability. In theory, such a tool ought to encourage the user to perform a thorough and comprehensive security audit on the organisation's information systems, and ought not to produce too much paperwork as a result. Tool availability is likely to change as the standard is more widely taken up and any organisation interested in pursuing this route should, therefore, do up-to-date research on what is available before making a shortlist.

The organisation may need to compare tools before making a selection and should concentrate, in the comparison process, on the extent to which the tool really does easily and effectively automate the risk assessment and Statement of Applicability development process, the amount of additional paperwork it generates, the flexibility it offers for dealing with changing circumstances and frequent, smaller scale risk assessments, and the meaningfulness of the results it generates.

Tracking changes to the risk assessment process over time is also of importance, and often the 'future-proofing' aspect of requirements of the tool are overlooked during the initial purchase because of the focus on achieving certification, or at least the implementation of an ISO27001-compliant ISMS. Of course, normal due diligence analyses should also be undertaken into the status of the supplier and manufacturer of the product to ensure that it is properly supported and likely to continue to be.

Risk assessments can be done without using such tools, although it can be difficult to demonstrate that the risk assessment produces comparable and reproducible results without using such a tool. A proper risk assessment in any business will be very time consuming, whether or not a software tool is used. 'Time consuming' means one or more months of dedicated work and, for larger organisations, even longer. The use of a software tool will depend on the culture of the organisation and the preferences of the information security adviser and manager.

Practically speaking, once the organisation has decided to purchase such a tool, it becomes dependent on that tool and on the staff members who are trained to use it. In considering the appropriate route forward, consideration should be given to the likelihood of being able to recruit staff who have broad risk assessment experience and can adapt to the organisation's environment as against the likelihood of recruiting and retaining staff who have specific experience with one risk assessment tool, if that tool requires particular specialist knowledge.

If the organisation decides to purchase such a tool, the ISMS project steering group should document the reasons for its choice and selection. Whoever is to use it will, of course, have to be fully competent in its use. Evidence of any training and of the level of proficiency achieved should be retained on the personnel file of the person trained in its use.

It is essential to appreciate that risk assessment tools are a specific type of tool, different from other tools, such as gap analysis tools, vulnerability assessment tools or penetration testing, each of which is briefly described before we provide guidance on current risk assessment tools.

Gap analysis tools

It is important to understand the difference between a gap analysis and an ISO27001-compliant risk assessment. A risk assessment is individual asset-based; a gap analysis assesses the gap between the requirements of a standard or other set of requirements (such as a risk treatment plan or Statement of Applicability) and the controls that are actually in place. Such gap analysis tools almost invariably analyse the gap between the controls in place in an organisation and the complete set of those required by the standard. While this exercise can be interesting, it is not deeply useful.

This is because, where ISO27001 is concerned, not all organisations are likely to need to implement all the controls identified in the standard; an analysis of the gap between the requirements of the standard and the current implementation status is not, therefore, particularly useful in the creation of an ISO27001-compliant ISMS. In our analysis, where something identified by the vendor as a 'risk assessment tool' is patently only a gap analysis tool, we have clearly identified it as such. There is no point in attempting to use such a tool to carry out the risk assessment component of the ISMS project, because it simply doesn't meet the requirements of the standard.

Vulnerability assessment tools

Vulnerability assessment tools,[28] also called security scanning tools, are also not risk assessment tools as defined by the standard. They may well be used as part of the risk

---

[28] See the discussion, in Chapter 9, on technical vulnerability controls.

assessment process, in order to identify vulnerabilities. They do have a role to play in many information security management systems, and that role is determined by the risk treatment plan which arises from the risk assessment. Vulnerability assessment tools assess the security of network or host systems and report system vulnerabilities. These tools are designed to scan networks, servers, firewalls, routers and software applications for vulnerabilities. Generally, the tools can detect known security flaws or bugs in software and hardware, determine if the systems are susceptible to known attacks and exploits, and search for system vulnerabilities, such as settings contrary to established security policies.

In evaluating a vulnerability assessment tool, consider how frequently it is updated to include the detection of new weaknesses, security flaws and bugs, and whether or not it refers to common lists of flaws and vulnerabilities, such as the SANS Top Cyber Security Risks, CVE and Bugtraq.[29] Vulnerability assessment tools are not usually run in real-time, but are commonly run on a periodic basis. The tools can generate both technical and management reports, including text, charts and graphs. Vulnerability assessment reports can identify what weaknesses exist and how to fix them.

Penetration testing

Penetration testing (or pentesting) is also not a risk assessment. A penetration analysis is a snapshot of the

---

[29] For SANS, CVE and Bugtraq, see the website references in the footnotes on p 109, below.

organisation's security at a specific point in time. It can test the effectiveness of security controls and preparedness measures. Whilst a vulnerability assessment is usually an automated process, using a vulnerability assessment tool, penetration testing usually involves a team of (external) experts who test and identify an information system's vulnerability to attack. They may attempt to bypass security controls by exploiting identified vulnerabilities including, for instance, social engineering, denial of service attacks and other methods. The objective of a penetration analysis is to locate system vulnerabilities so that appropriate corrective steps can be taken.

Pentesting does, therefore, have a role to play in the ISO27001 risk assessment; it has an even more substantial role to play after the assessment, to test the effectiveness of defences that have been installed and to ensure that technical controls are performing as they are expected to.

Risk assessment tools

Not all of those tools that currently claim to be ISO27001 risk assessment tools are necessarily so, and those that are may in any case not meet your requirements. Different tools target different organisational profiles and are sold under various licence arrangements. Aspects that should be considered in determining the most suitable tool for any one project should include:

- the platform the tool is to run on (laptop, server, ASP server, etc.);

- scope of compliance of the standard (ISO/IEC 27001:2005, ISO/IEC 27002:2005, NIST SP 800-30, PCI standard, etc.);

- scalability (to the needs of the organisation and to the number of users);

- flexibility (the ability to divide the process into various sections and run them as discreet assessments in their own right, e.g. for business units, or for specific IT systems, or after change to an asset, and then the option to analyse the wider impact on full assessment);

- import (of, for instance, asset lists) and export facility;

- customisable reporting, to suit organisational structures;

- degree of alignment with ISO27001 or with establishing an ISMS (especially any support in producing a Statement of Applicability);

- licence model;

- ease of use (because the more training that is required the higher the total cost of ownership, particularly when you consider back-up expertise);

- price; and

- any requirements for integrating the risk assessment results with another risk management regime.

We have identified the following software tools, each of which claims (to one extent or another) to be an information security risk assessment tool:

- Callio Secura, from Callio Technologies

  www.callio.com

- COBRA

  www.riskworld.net

- CRAMM, in the UK from Siemens

www.cramm.com

- Ezrisk

- ISRAC, from Infosecure Group

  www.infosecuregroup.com

- Proteus

  www.infogov.com

- PTA (Practical Threat Analysis)

  www.ptatechnologies.com

- RA2 art of risk

  www.aexis.de

- RiskWatch

  www.riskwatch.com

- RSAM, from Relational Security

  www.relsec.com

- vsRisk™

  www.vigilantsoftware.co.uk

OAT (the OCTAVE Automated Tool) for users of OCTAVE is designed to respond exclusively to the US NIST SP 800-26[30] standard and has, therefore, not been considered in this book.

---

[30] NIST SP 800-26, *Security Self-Assessment Guide for Information Technology Systems*, was published in 2001 and contains questions designed to enable 'agency officials to determine the current status of their information security programs'.

Risk assessment tool descriptions[31]

Callio's tool, Callio Secura, is a team-oriented tool that has been built around ISO17799:2000 and BS7799-2:2002. It is web-based, which brings with it specific risks that it has not apparently been optimised to control. It contains sample policies, a document manager, an employee awareness centre, a very limited risk assessment tool and a more comprehensive gap analysis tool. It does not perform a risk assessment as required by the standard. More importantly, it appears not to have been updated for ISO27001 and it still contains the control structure of ISO17799:2000, which was withdrawn in 2005. It does not look as though it would be even vaguely useful for organisations seeking certification to the current standard.

Cobra (release 3) is a gap analysis tool (it claims to do an ISO17799 compliance check), not a risk assessment tool, and it appears not to support either risk management or the establishment of the ISMS; at US$895 it's an expensive gap analysis tool.

CRAMM is the oldest risk assessment tool. Version 5 is the current version. It is the preferred tool of the UK government and is recommended by them for use in the public sector. It is widely available through Insight Consulting in the UK and its agents in other countries. It has two modules (CRAMM Express and CRAMM Expert). It provides:

- risk assessment and management methods;

---

[31] The information contained in this section is derived from our own research. Within the limitations of research carried out in a competitive market place, it was valid at the time of the assessment. We emphasise that these are our own assessments; any reader who wishes to review the tools is encouraged to do so.

- business continuity planning support;

- ISO27001 compliance gap analysis, security improvement programme, Statement of Applicability and risk treatment reporting; and

- a database of over 3,000 security controls.

The reports CRAMM runs cannot be altered, but there are many pre-defined reports, including:

- Measures of Risk Report, Risk Assessment Report, Risk Management Report;

- Countermeasures Status Report and Countermeasures Cost Report; and

- What-If Report.

In support of ISO27001 it also offers reports for:

- Information Security Policy;

- Scope of ISMS;

- Gap Analysis; and

- Statement of Applicability.

CRAMM appears to meet the key requirements that were set out earlier in this chapter. The customisability of its reports and interfaces is, however, a bit limited. There are two versions available: 'Express' (£1,500 plus £250 annual licence) and 'Expert' (£2,950 plus £875 annual licence). Siemens can deploy its consultancy expertise to help customise the Expert version and it recommends that anyone who will be using the tool should undergo their three-day (£1,195) non-residential training programme. It is not, in other words, necessarily as easy to use as they would like it to be. It is, though, the sort of tool that no ISO27001 auditor will object to.

Ezrisk is a risk assessment tool, but is not ISO27001:2005 compliant and its ISO module appears to be more of a gap analysis tool than a risk assessment one.

ISRAC is available in business and enterprise versions and works with ISO17799, not ISO27001. However, it carries out risk assessments at the business process level, not the asset level, and it, therefore, fails the first requirement of an ISO27001-compliant risk assessment tool. The fact that it treats physical security as an area different from information security (and, therefore, offers a second module for assessing physical security risks) indicates a fundamental non-conformance to an essential point of the standard, which is that all information, both digital and analogue, has to be protected and that physical controls are as important as logical ones.

Proteus appears to be mainly an ISO27001 compliance gap analysis tool. There are various versions available. It does not appear to contain an ISO27001 risk management function. Costs vary from approximately £600 plus licence fee/arrangements upwards.

PTA is a risk assessment tool, but was originally designed for use in system specification and does not appear to be ISO27001 compatible in any way. Anyone who wished to use it for an ISO27001 deployment would probably have to invest an uneconomic level of time in customising this product.

RiskWatch meets many of the requirements identified earlier in this chapter. It has an effective, comprehensive risk assessment methodology and can assess risk both quantitatively and qualitatively. While it was not built specifically for ISO27001 work, or the establishment and management of an ISMS, it claims that it can apply both ISO27002 and NIST SP 800-26[32] controls and can be either PC or server-based. While it appears to be a first-class tool, it is also by far the most expensive. A single user licence costs US$14,500. It is probably best suited to larger organisations that require a more sophisticated and granular approach to risk quantification, and to organisations with a US exposure (or that are based in North America), because NIST SP 800-26 compliance is not a requirement outside the US. It is also useful to risk consultants whose offering includes sophisticated, detailed risk assessments at this level.

RSAM is a comprehensive, scalable, multi-standard, multi-user, client-server gap analysis tool. It doesn't follow ISO27001 methodology and it doesn't produce a Statement of Applicability. It's not likely to help with an ISMS project.

RA2 was developed by two consultants who were deeply involved in both the 2005 revision to ISO27002 and the development of ISO27001. Their risk assessment tool is absolutely in line with the process required by the standard and it can be purchased online. The risk assessment methodology is qualitative and is also in line with the standard. While it is effective for an organisation's initial risk assessment, it is not as obviously capable of comparing assessments and control recommendations made at different times, nor does it easily allow uploading of individual asset details. These two characteristics mean that it is best suited

---

[32] NIST SP 800-26, *Security Self-Assessment Guide for Information Technology Systems.*

to small to medium organisations, carrying out their first risk assessment as part of their initial ISMS project. It is not self-explanatory to use, but there is no requirement for offsite user training. At £1,100 for a single user licence, it is about half the price of the Expert version of CRAMM. There is no enterprise version.

vsRisk™ This tool has been designed specifically for ISO27001 risk assessments, but also supports ISO27002. Uniquely, it is also in line with the guidelines of BS7799-3 and ISO27005, and both NIST SP 800-26 and SP 800-30. It is also in line with the requirements of the ISF[33] Security Standard 2005 and the Risk Management Standard, developed jointly by the UK's major risk management organisations.[34] It was developed by a specialist risk management software company[35] to a project brief prepared by the authors of this book, and worldwide marketing rights are held by Vigilant Software™ Ltd. The features of vsRisk™ include:

- a wizard-based approach to simplify and accelerate the process for undertaking risk assessments;

- asset-by-asset identification of threats and vulnerabilities;

- a process to assign all relevant ISO27001 Annex A controls;

---

[33] Information Security Forum, a members-only organisation whose Standard of Information Security Good Practice is available from www.securityforum.org.

[34] The contributors to the Risk Management Standard were the IRM (Institute of Risk Management), AIRMIC (the Association of Insurance and Risk Managers) and ALARM (the National Forum for Risk Management in the Public Sector).

[35] Top Solutions (UK) Ltd , who developed, marketed and supported award-winning risk management software.

- easily imports additional controls to deal with additional risks;

- integrated ISO27005-compliant threat and vulnerability databases, which are continually updated to ensure that they are the most up-to-date available anywhere, with one year of free updates built into the price);

- customisable management scale and risk acceptance criteria;

- helps define the scope and business requirements, policy and objectives for the ISMS;

- produces an audit-ready Statement of Applicability;

- detailed gap analysis helps drive forward the risk treatment plan;

- integrated audit trail and comparative history;

- helps develop an ISMS asset inventory;

- captures business, legal and contractual requirements against each asset;

- ability to assess confidentiality, integrity and availability against each asset;

- in-built intuitive help feature;

- asset monitor supports import and export of asset information;

- backup and restore capability;

- simplifies a business-critical but complex task – meaning external training is not required.

It has been designed with the aim of supporting an ISO27001-compliant risk assessment beyond the first implementation PDCA cycle and has a clear user interface. It does the ISO27001 risk assessment job correctly, easily and efficiently.

Conclusions

CRAMM, with its pedigree, is the cautious choice, but is not the easiest or most user-friendly of risk assessment tools. RiskWatch might be the sophisticate's choice, but the return on investment ratio needs to be carefully calculated, and ISO27001 compliance is not in-built.

RA2 is a tool that complies with ISO27001, and at a reasonable price.

Our view, however, is that, for most organisations, and for consultants providing ISMS services to most organisations, the most appropriate tool – in terms of functionality, ease of use and value for money – is the one that is completely in line with the requirements of ISO27001, as well as all other national and international standards on information security risk assessment, and that is vsRisk™.

CHAPTER 6: INFORMATION SECURITY POLICY AND SCOPING[36]

While risk assessment is the core competence of information security, it is the information security policy and the agreed scope of the ISMS that provide the organisational context within which that risk assessment takes place. The first step in the planning phase for the establishment of an ISMS is the definition of the information security policy. A risk assessment can only be carried out once an information security policy exists to provide context and direction for the risk assessment activity.

Information security policy

This requirement is set out in clause 4.2.1 of ISO27001[37] (and control A.5.1, in Annex A to ISO27001). It is not always, however, as straightforward as it seems. It may be an iterative process (particularly in complex organisations

---

[36] Much of this chapter replicates (but does not replace) content that is already in *IT Governance: a Manager's Guide to Data Security and ISO 27001/ISO 27002* (Kogan Page, 2007), as well as *International IT Governance: an Executive Guide to ISO 27001/ISO 17799* (Kogan Page, 2006), and is repeated here to provide context for the further contents of this book. Readers are encouraged to read the original books for the full value of the contents of this chapter.

[37] Readers who do not already have copies of both ISO/IEC 27001:2005 and ISO/IEC 27002:2005 should obtain their own copies and read them. The standards are the key documents against which an accredited certification is carried out. Copies of the standards (in either paper or downloadable format) can be obtained from national standards bodies and from the IT Governance online shop (at *www.itgovernance.co.uk/standards.aspx*).

dealing with complex information security issues and/or multiple domains) and the final form of security policy that is adopted may, therefore, have to reflect the final risk assessment that has been carried out and the Statement of Applicability which emerges from that.

Clause 4.2.1 sets out clearly the components of the ISMS policy. Its scope, and the policy itself, must take into account the characteristics of the business, its organisation, location, assets and technology. The policy must include a framework for setting its objectives and establish the overall sense of direction. It must take into account all relevant business, legal, regulatory and contractual security requirements. It must establish the strategic context (for the organisation and for its approach to risk management) within which the ISMS will be established. It must establish criteria for the evaluation of risk, for the structure of the risk assessment, and for risk treatment decisions. It must be formally approved by senior management.

A statement that the board and management 'are committed to preserving the confidentiality, integrity and availability of information' will be at the heart of a security policy and an ISMS. It is important to define precisely the key terms used in the policy and we recommend that the definitions contained in ISO27001 and, where necessary, in ISO27002 are used. The introduction to ISO27002 defines information very widely:

Information [can be] printed or written on paper, stored electronically, transmitted by post or using electronic means, shown on films, [or] spoken in conversation.

In other words, appropriate protection is required for *all* forms of information.

Confidentiality [is defined in clause 3.1 of the standard as] ensuring that information is accessible only to those authorized to have access.

Integrity [is defined as] safeguarding the accuracy and completeness of information and processing methods by protecting against unauthorized modification.

Availability [is defined as] ensuring that authorized users have access to information and associated assets when required.

Availability is particularly important to businesses engaged in e-commerce. A business that depends for its very existence on the availability of its website, but which fails to take adequate steps to ensure that the site is up, running and running properly at all times, is likely to fail as a business much more quickly than a traditional bricks and mortar business that is unable to open its shop doors for a few days.

The board, management team and staff of the organisation should all understand that these are the definitions of these words and they should be prominently set out in the early briefings to staff and in internal communications. Auditors from certification bodies are likely to check (probably randomly) that staff understand what these words mean and, while they will not look for staff to remember verbatim these definitions, will want staff to demonstrate a practical understanding of how the pursuit of these aspects of information security is likely to impact their own work. This level of understanding is required, as a minimum, so that each member of staff is able to recognise and react appropriately to a security incident.

The organisation will also need to define which physical and intellectual assets are to be covered by the policy. The kinds of technology employed and the basis on which the organisation operates will also strongly influence the scope of the ISMS.

The information security policy will also have to be regularly reviewed and updated in the light of changing circumstances, environment and experience. As a minimum, if there is no earlier reason for the board to review its policy, it should be reviewed annually and the board should agree that the policy remains appropriate (or otherwise) to its needs in the light of any changes to the business context, the risk assessment criteria or in the identified risks. There may be components of the policy that ought to be reviewed very regularly, even monthly, and these should be identified through the risk assessment.

Initially, the information security policy is a short statement (we think organisations should aim for a maximum of two pages of A4) that is designed to set out clearly the strategic aims and control objectives that will guide the development of the ISMS. The policy may go through a number of stages of development, particularly in the light of the risk assessment, but the final version must satisfy clause 4.2.1 – and Annex A control 5.1.1 – of ISO27001, as well as appropriately reflecting the good practice that is set out in clause 5 of ISO27002. The guidance in the introduction to ISO27002 should also have been read and taken into account.[38] Proof that the policy has been approved by management, published and communicated internally, and that it is reviewed regularly (usually annually, as a minimum), with any changes similarly published and

---

[38] The information security policy template that is contained within the ISO27001 ISMS Documentation Toolkit is drafted specifically to meet all these requirements and, like other top-level documents within the toolkit, needs minimal adaptation to meet the needs of individual organisations (see *www.itgovernance.co.uk/free_trial.aspx*).

communicated, will enable the organisation to fully satisfy control A.5.1 of the standard (Security Policy).

A copy of that section of the minutes (preferably initialled by the chairman as a correct copy) of the board meeting, in which the information security policy was debated and adopted, should be filed with the security policy documentation. It can be a controlled document and it does, for audit purposes, provide useful and immediate evidence of the process by which the policy was adopted, and of any amendments to it. This, together with the proposal that was put to the board, is the first part of the evidence that clause 4.3 (Documentation Requirements) of the standard requires to demonstrate that the actions set out in clause 4.2 did take place.

The policy itself should then be issued as a controlled document and made available to all who fall within its scope; as a minimum, members of the senior management team should receive individual copies and copies should be posted on all internal noticeboards, both the physical and electronic ones. These copies of the policy document should, of course, be clearly marked as controlled copies, to ensure that they are updated to reflect any changes that take place. Copies handed out, as part of training or awareness seminars, should be marked as uncontrolled copies.

Scope of the ISMS

Those parts of the organisation, and possibly beyond, to which the policy is going to apply, need to be clearly identified. This may be done in part on the basis of corporate, divisional or management structure, or on the basis of geographic location. The other aspect of scope that needs to be considered is the logical boundary. A virtual organisation, or a dispersed, multi-site operation, may have different security issues from one located on a single site. In practical terms, a security policy that encompasses all of the activities within a specific entity, for which a specific board of directors or management team is responsible, is more easily implemented than one that is to be applied to only part of the entity. It is important to ensure that the board of directors that is implementing the policy does actually have adequate control over the operations specified within the policy and that it will be able to give a clear mandate to its management team to implement it.

It is essential to decide the boundary within which the ISMS is to provide assurance. The business environment and the Internet are each so huge and diverse that it is necessary to draw a boundary between what is within the organisation and what is without. In simple terms, boundaries are physically or logically identifiable. Boundaries have to be identified in terms of the organisation, or part of the organisation, that is to be protected, which networks and which data, and at which geographic locations.

The key components of defining the scope of the ISMS are:

- identifying the boundaries or perimeters (physical and logical) of what is to be protected;

- identifying all the systems necessary for the reception, storage, manipulation and transmission of information or data within those boundaries and the information assets within those systems;

- identifying the relationships between these systems, the information assets and the organisational objectives and tasks;

- identifying the systems and information assets that are critical to the achievement of these organisational objectives and tasks and, if possible, ranking them in order of priority.

Clause A.7.1 is the ISO27001 Annex A control that deals with the asset inventory and the guidance of clause 7.1 of ISO27002:2005 should be taken at this point. It identifies clearly the classes or types of information asset that should be considered, and recommends that the information security classification of the asset be determined at this time – which would be sensible, given the requirement of control A.7.2 for information to be appropriately classified.

The first step, therefore, is to identify which organisational entity is within the scope of the ISMS. The entity that is within the scope must be capable of physical and/or logical separation from third parties and from other organisations within a larger group. While this does not exclude third party contractors, it does make it practically very difficult (although not necessarily impossible) to put an ISMS in place within an organisation that shares significant network and/or information assets or geographic locations. A division of a larger organisation that, for instance, shares a group head office and head office functions with other divisions, could not practically implement a meaningful ISMS.

Usually, the smallest organisational entity that is capable of implementing an ISMS is one that is self-contained. It will have its own board of directors or management team, its own functional support, its own premises and its own IT network.

The information that should be collected (following NIST SP 800-30, clause 3.1.1), in order to clarify what will – and what won't – be within the scope of the ISMS, will relate to:

- hardware;
- software;
- system interfaces (e.g. internal and external connectivity);
- data and information;
- persons who support and use the IT systems;
- system mission (i.e. the processes performed by the systems);
- system and data criticality (e.g. the system's value or importance to the organisation);
- system and data sensitivity;
- functional requirements of the IT system;
- users of the system (e.g. system users who provide technical support to the IT system, application users who use the IT system to perform business functions);
- system security policies governing the IT system;
- system security architecture;
- current network topology (e.g. network diagram);
- information storage protection;

- flow of information pertaining to the IT system (e.g. system interfaces, system input and output flow charts);

- technical controls used in the IT system;

- management controls used in the IT system;

- operational controls used in the IT system;

- physical security environment of the IT system;

- environmental security implemented for the IT system.

Information gathered about some or all of these issues will help clarify what should be in the scope of the ISMS.

It is possible for divisions of larger organisations to independently pursue certification. The critical factor is the extent to which they can be practically differentiated from other divisions of the same parent organisation, and can exercise practical control over their information assets and over the implementation of controls which their risk assessment determines are necessary to protect those assets.

For larger organisations, with a multiplicity of systems and extensive geographic spread, it is as a general rule often simpler to tackle ISO27001 and, in particular, risk assessment, on the basis of smaller business units that meet the general description set out above. On the other hand, larger organisations that have a single business culture and largely common systems throughout are probably better off creating a single ISMS.

Once the organisational scope is identified, it is necessary to list the physical premises that the chosen organisation occupies and to identify its network and information assets.

It is critical, if there are aspects of the organisation's activities or systems that are to be excluded from the requirements of the security policy, that these are clearly identified – and explained – at this stage. Multi-site or virtual organisations will need to carefully consider the different security requirements of their different sites and their management implications. There should be clear boundaries (defined in terms of the characteristics of the organisation, its location, assets and technology) within which the security policy and ISMS will apply.

Any exclusions should be openly debated by the board and the steering group and the minutes should set out how and why the decision – for or against – was taken. It is possible that, in fact, divisions of the organisation, components of the information system or specific assets will not be able to be excluded from the scope, either because they are already so integral to it, or because their exclusion might have the effect of undermining the information security objectives themselves. It must, therefore, be clear that any exclusions do not, in any way, undermine the security of the organisation to be assessed.

Certification auditors will be assessing how management applies its information security policy across the whole of the organisation that is defined as being within the scope of the policy. They should be expected to test to their limits the boundaries of the stated scope to ensure that all interdependencies and points of weakness have been identified and adequately dealt with.

In reality, as stated earlier, the process of designing and implementing an effective ISMS may be made simpler by including, within the scope, the entire organisation for which the board has responsibility.

There is an argument, in large, complex organisations, for a phased approach to implementation. Where it really is possible to adequately define a subsidiary part of the organisation, such that its information security needs can be independently assessed, it may be possible to gain substantial experience in designing and implementing an ISMS, as well as a track record of success and the momentum that accompanies it, so that a subsequent roll-out to the rest of the organisation can be carried through successfully and smoothly. These considerations apply to any large, complex project and the appropriate answer depends very much on individual organisational circumstances.

It would certainly be a mistake to define the scope too narrowly. While it may appear, on the surface, that this is a route to a quick and easy certification, it is in fact, a route to a worthless certificate. Any external party, assessing the nature of an organisation's ISMS, will want to be sure that all the critical functions that may affect its relationship are included and a limited scope will not do this. We are aware that some certification organisations are prepared to consider scopes that cover less than a complete business unit and, in our opinion, they are doing a disservice to their clients, as well as to the integrity of the ISO27001 scheme. Do not be tempted by such certification bodies to pursue an approach which is likely to be inadequate to your long term needs.

The other issue with regards to scope, and that directly relates to the risk management aspects of the project, as well as the project in general, is how it maps onto management responsibilities at the top level. The scope of the ISMS should be aligned with the boundaries of a single management team's responsibility. This should be the management team that has authority to sign the information security policy and has responsibility for directing and managing the organisation that falls within the scope. This means that when it comes to deciding on the acceptable level of risk it is just one person, or group (e.g. board or management team) who decide, and this is demonstrated by one individual signing off the relevant documentation. Of course, it also helps with the smooth progress of the project in general when all those who will contribute fall within the remit of one, dedicated management team.

The overall issue of scoping is certainly one where experienced, professional support can be helpful in assessing the best way forward.

CHAPTER 7: THE ISO27001 RISK ASSESSMENT

We've already looked at the ISO27001 risk assessment in the context of the ERM framework and in relation to the PDCA cycle. This chapter provides an overview of the steps that ISO27001 specifically requires, identifies some gaps, and introduces the additional best practice guidance available in ISO27002, ISO27005 and BS7799-3:2006 (BS7799).[39]

We want to remind readers, at this point, that there is an important difference between a specification and a code of practice. A specification, such as ISO27001, sets out specific requirements which, if followed, will allow a management system to receive a third party certificate of conformity. A code of practice, such as ISO27002 or ISO27005, provides guidance on best practice, but sets out no specific requirements against which a management system can be audited. It is not possible, therefore, for there to be a certificate of conformance with a code of practice.

ISO27001 contains a specification for the key steps in a risk assessment. Organisations seeking accredited certification to ISO27001 must – as a minimum – follow these steps. There are no other options. This is not a code of practice – it is a specification, a statement of requirements. You can do more than ISO27001 specifies and, in some areas, you'll find that you need to – but you must, at the very least, do what is required.

---

[39] BS7799-3:2006 *Information Security Management Systems – Part 3: Guidelines for information security risk management*; see *www.itgovernance.co.uk/products/162*.

A code of practice does provide useful guidance. It is not mandatory to follow the guidance, but there is some sense in taking advantage of work that has already been done in order to achieve better results, more quickly. You should remember, though, that whatever guidance you might turn to, no matter how useful it appears, it is the standard itself that counts. No matter what other experts, or even this book, suggest, it is ISO27001 itself that defines the one and only set of requirements that need to be met in order to develop and deploy an ISMS capable of accredited certification. The auditor should always turn to a copy of ISO27001 first and last in order to confirm what its requirements are.

ISO27002, ISO27005 and BS7799-3 are codes of practice. ISO27005 primarily provides best practice guidance on the implementation of the 133 controls that are in Annex A of ISO27001, but it does also provide limited guidance on risk assessment, some of which is useful in developing a risk assessment methodology. ISO27005 and BS7799-3, on the other hand, deal specifically with risk assessment and are sensible sources of additional information and guidance on areas in which ISO27001 is silent, but on which decisions will be required if the ISMS is to work in detail.

Overview of the risk assessment process

ISO27001 says that, first of all, 'criteria against which risk will be evaluated' must be contained within the ISMS policy (4.2.1 - b3). Within the context provided by the policy, the organisation must identify a suitable risk assessment methodology that takes into account identified business, information security, legal and regulatory requirements (4.2.1 - c1) and that the criteria for accepting

6.1.2(b)

risks and for identifying the acceptable level of risks are defined (4.2.1 - c2).

ISO27001 provides no guidance as to how an 'acceptable level of risk' should be defined.

While it is crystal clear on the steps that are required in the risk assessment, ISO27001 also provides no guidance as to what risk assessment methodology should be adopted although, as we said in Chapter 2, the expectation is that it will be a qualitative one. The standard is clear: the criteria against which risks should be evaluated should be established before the risk assessment is undertaken.

7.1(a)

ISO27001 says that the organisation's risk assessment methodology (which should reflect the organisation's risk appetite and/or sit within the existing ERM structure, as we discussed earlier and as required by clause 4.2.1 - b3) must produce 'comparable and reproducible results' (clause 4.2.1 - c). This means that once the first risk assessment has been done, any subsequent risk assessments can be compared to it as a baseline or benchmark. As a consequence of this, once controls have been applied in the light of the risk treatment decision, the risk assessment could be repeated and the remaining, residual risks could be confirmed as being within the organisation's level of risk tolerance and that, therefore, the ISMS is effective and the information security policy objectives are being achieved.

Once the risk assessment methodology has been defined, work can get under way. The precise risk assessment steps are that the organisation:

- identifies the assets (i.e. anything that has value to the organisation) within the scope of the ISMS, and the owners of those assets (clause 4.2.1 - d1);

6.1.2(c)(2)

- identifies the business, legal and contractual requirements that are relevant to the identified assets;[40]

- values the identified assets, taking into account the confidentiality, availability and integrity of the assets in each of their business, legal and contractual contexts;

- identifies the threats to the identified assets (4.2.1 - d2);

- identifies the vulnerabilities that might be exploited by those threats (4.2.1 - d3);

- analyses the impacts that losses of confidentiality, integrity and availability may have on each of the assets in each of their business, legal and contractual contexts (4.2.1 - d4);

- assesses the 'realistic likelihood' of these impacts occurring (4.2.1 - e2); and

- estimates the risks to the assets, using these factors (clause 4.2.1 - e3).

This estimation of the level of risk – what we call the 'risk equation' and which we discuss further, below – is achieved by first assessing the business, legal/regulatory and contractual impacts on the organisation of security failures (taking into account the consequences of a loss of confidentiality, integrity or availability), then assessing the realistic likelihood of the failure occurring for the given threats and vulnerabilities and (where appropriate) the controls currently implemented.

---

[40] While this and the subsequent step are not clearly mandated by ISO27001, the requirement of clause 4.2.1 - b2 'takes into account business and legal or regulatory requirements, and contractual security obligations' can only practically be met by addressing them at this point. This approach is precisely in line with the recommendations of BS7799-3, clause 5.3.

The relationship between these attributes is reflected in the diagram below. It assumes that there is an estimable likelihood that an identified threat will exploit an identified vulnerability; if it does, there will be an estimable impact and the product of impact and likelihood gives rise to the risk level. Whether or not that level of risk is acceptable depends entirely on the organisation's risk acceptance criteria.

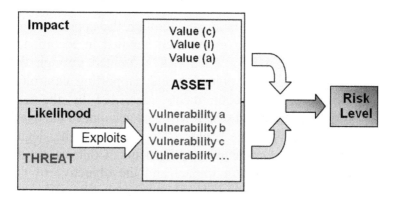

Figure 8: Sources of the risk equation

Clause 4.2.1 - e4 of ISO27001 then requires the organisation to determine which of these risks are acceptable and which require treatment in light of the criteria set out at the start of the process (at 4.2.1 - c).

The standard then requires you to 'identify and evaluate' options for the treatment of the risks (4.2.1 - f) and provides four possible headline options for this treatment. These are in line with our description in an earlier chapter and are to:

- knowingly accept the risks, providing they satisfy the organisation's policies and risk acceptance criteria, i.e.

they are within its level of risk tolerance or risk appetite; or

- apply appropriate controls (treating the risk) to reduce the risk to an acceptable level; or

- reject or avoid the risks, by, for example, finding a work-around; or

- transfer the business risks to other parties.

The risks that require treatment through the application of controls (option 2, above) are then handled in accordance with section 4.2.1 – g. Each risk is treated through the selection of a control objective and supporting control(s) that will meet the requirements identified by the risk assessment process and which will take account of the over-riding risk acceptance criteria, as well as the legal, regulatory and contractual requirements. Controls act to reduce likelihood and/or impact and the objective of the control selection process is to select controls that will bring the identified risk below the previously defined level of risk tolerance, as shown in the risk treatment matrix opposite:

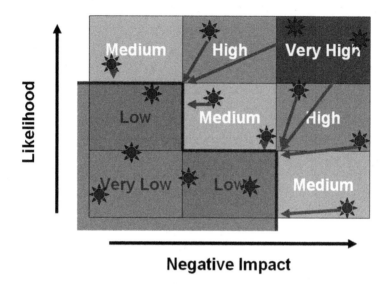

Negative Impact

Figure 9: Controls reduce impact and/or likelihood to bring the risk down to the level of risk tolerance/acceptance

The penultimate step in the 'plan' stage of the initial ISO27001 Plan-Do-Check-Act cycle is the production of a Statement of Applicability, the list of all the controls identified in Annex A of ISO27001 and a statement (together with a justification) as to whether or not that control has been applied within the organisation's ISMS.

Formal management approval is then required for the Statement of Applicability, for the proposed residual risks, and for the implementation of the selected controls and operation of the ISMS.

Let's now take a more detailed look at each of the key stages in the risk assessment process.

CHAPTER 8: INFORMATION ASSETS

The information security policy and the scoping statement, discussed in Chapter 6, describe the boundaries of the ISMS. You have to consider, at a reasonably high level, the information assets that underpin the organisation's business processes in order to establish the scope of the ISMS. You now return to the subject, but this time the objective is to identify all those assets in detail.

Assets within the scope

The first step in meeting the ISO27001 requirements for risk assessments is to identify all the information assets (and 'assets' includes information systems – which should be so defined in your information security policy) within the scope (4.2.1 - a) of the ISMS and, at the same time, to document which individual and/or department 'owns' the asset. We discuss, in Chapter 10, the valuation of assets, particularly in relation to their business, legal/regulatory and contractual requirements.

This asset identification exercise can only take place once the scope – discussed in Chapter 6 – has been finalised.

Asset classes

ISO27002 identifies, in A.7.1.1, the six classes of assets that have to be considered, each of which should be referenced in your information security policy statement. These asset classes include the asset types we discussed in

Chapter 6 and should frame your asset identification exercise. They are as follows:

- **Information assets:** this category includes information printed or written on paper, transmitted by post, shown in films, or spoken in conversation, as well as information stored electronically on servers, website(s), extranet(s), intranet(s), PCs, laptops, mobile phones and PDAs as well as on CD-ROMs, floppy disks, USB sticks, backup tapes and any other digital or magnetic media, and information transmitted electronically by any means. It includes databases and data files, contracts and agreements, system documentation, research information, user manuals, training material, operational or support procedures, business continuity plans, fallback arrangements, audit trails, and archived information.

- **Software:** which includes the sets of instructions that tell the system(s) how to manipulate information (i.e. the software: operating systems, applications, development tools, utilities, etc.).

- **Physical assets and hardware** on which the information is manipulated: such as the computer and communications equipment (including, for instance, laptops, mobile phones, PDAs, etc.), removable media (e.g. USB sticks, CD-ROMs, backup tapes, etc.) and infrastructure assets, such as server rooms, copper cables and fibre circuits.

- **Services** on which computer systems depend: computing and communications services, and general utilities such as heating, lighting, power and air-conditioning (burglar alarms might also be included).

- **People:** who carry much information in their heads, and the qualifications, skills and experience that is necessary for their interaction with the organisation's data.

- **Intangibles:** such as intellectual property, reputation, brand image, etc.

There should be a link between this inventory and the organisation's fixed asset ledger and/or its configuration management database (CMDB), and the sensitivity classification (as required by ISO27001 Annex A clause 7) of every asset, together with details of its owner, which should be recorded as well.

One of the exercises that we do in our Masterclasses[41] is to analyse the information assets that are contained on the average workstation or laptop. These are likely to include, apart from the hardware itself (and, possibly, various peripheral hardware items such as keyboards, mice, etc.) the operating system, individual applications such as e-mail software, word processing and spreadsheet software, and a number of other specific applications, as well as databases, customer records, other contact records, copies of important information, files, folders, e-mail databases, and so on. Each of these assets may have a different classification level, and not all of the assets will necessarily be owned by the user of the workstation.

The objective of the corporate asset identification exercise is to analyse assets down to the level of granularity suggested by our training exercise. A usual starting point is with the key corporate information systems or bodies of information. A system consists of a number of components.

---

[41] See *www.itgovernance.co.uk/products/291*.

A single data asset (such as a file, whether electronic or paper) is a component of a system.

These systems will include a number of IT systems (e.g. client relationship management system, payroll system, e-mail system, resource planning system, accounting system, etc.), the telecommunications systems and the paperwork filing systems. The risk analysis team should list the key systems throughout the organisation; there are software tools (for network mapping and software asset management, for instance) that can be used to ensure that all the data assets and all the IT systems have been identified. It might be necessary to deploy software tools to identify all the hardware and software that actually makes up the corporate infrastructure.

Telecommunications systems might include mobile phones as well as desk-based systems; personal digital assistants are as important a component of the IT system as are the remote access points and sub-contracted services.

The human resources filing system is as important as that used in the Chief Executive's or Chairman's office. All systems need to be identified and if, in the process of doing this, there are found to be significant sharings of assets or information sharings that were not identified earlier, then the scope of the ISMS may need to be revisited.

Grouping of assets

In most circumstances, it will be beneficial to group individual items and to treat that group as the 'asset' for the purposes of risk assessment. BS7799-3[42] says: 'Grouping similar or related assets into manageable collections can help to reduce the effort necessary for the risk assessment process' (clause 5.2). The key, here, is to ensure that the aggregation of assets into groups does not override the benefit of identifying threats and vulnerabilities at an individual asset level. For instance, it would not be helpful to aggregate all operating systems if the organisation's operating systems include multiple versions of Windows (e.g. NT4, Windows 2000 and Windows Vista) together with Linux and/or Unix, because the vulnerabilities – and therefore the threats – are likely to be different for each. Conversely, looking at all installations of Windows Vista together may be a sensible aggregation.

ISO27002, 7.1.2 identifies another such circumstance:

In complex information systems, it may be useful to designate groups of assets, which act together to provide a particular function, as 'services'. In this case, the service owner is responsible for the delivery of the service, including the functioning of the assets, which provide it.

Asset dependencies

In some cases, the dependency of one asset on another might affect the valuation of both assets and these dependencies should be identified during this phase of the project. For instance, if the integrity of data output from a program depends on the integrity of the data input, then the value of the second depends on that of the first. The

---

[42] ISO27005 unhelpfully simply says (at clause 8.2.1.2): 'Asset identification should be performed at a suitable level of detail that provides sufficient information for the risk assessment.'

integrity of the data might also be dependent on the availability of the power supply and the air conditioning. The confidentiality requirements of a specific data asset might require other assets, in which it is manipulated or stored, to be protected to a higher degree than might otherwise be the case.

ISO13335-3 (now withdrawn) provided helpful guidance here. Its suggestion is still useful:

- if the value of a dependent asset (e.g. data) is lower than or equal to the value of the asset (e.g. application software) on which it depends, then its value remains the same as it was; but

- if the value of the dependent asset is greater than that of the asset on which it depends, then its value should be increased in line with:

  - the degree of dependency, and
  - the values of other assets.

Asset owners[43]

Every asset must have an owner and this is reflected in Annex A control requirement A.7.1.2 (Ownership of Assets). In this instance the term 'owner' doesn't convey legal ownership of the asset to the individual and is defined (4.2.1 - d1, footnote 2) as the 'individual or entity that has approved management responsibility for controlling the production, development, maintenance, use and security of the assets'. This could, therefore, be a system administrator

---

[43] *Risk Assessment for Asset Owners* is a handy ITGP pocket guide expressly designed to guide asset owners in their contribution to the risk assessment.

or a manager who is responsible for defining how an asset or group of similar assets is used.

The owner of the asset is the person – or part of the business – who is responsible for appropriate classification and protection of the asset. In real terms, allocating ownership to a part of the organisation can be ineffective, unless that part has a clearly defined line of responsibility and individual accountability in place.

It is important to recognise that there may be a number of assets that have users, or custodians, who are not the nominated 'owners' of the asset: for instance, the operating system is likely to be owned by the system administrator, but it will be deployed on workstations throughout the organisation and will be used by workstation users. The system administrator will be responsible for the security (which, remember, includes availability as well as confidentiality and integrity) whereas the users are not accountable for these aspects. It may well be that, as a result of the risk assessment, specific controls (e.g. user access agreements) are imposed on the users.

Sensitivity classification

The asset owner is also responsible for determining the sensitivity classification of the asset. Control A.7.2.1 requires every information asset to be 'classified in terms of its value, legal requirements, sensitivity and criticality to the organization'. While there are comprehensive descriptions, elsewhere,[44] of how such guidelines should be

---

[44] See, specifically, Chapter 8 of *IT Governance: A Manager's Guide to Data Security and ISO 27001/ISO 27002*, Alan Calder and Steve G Watkins (Kogan Page, 2007).

developed and applied, there needs to be a direct relationship between the allocated sensitivity classification of an asset and the impact of its security being breached. We discuss impact valuations in Chapter 10. As a general guide, those assets that have a high impact valuation are likely to have a high sensitivity classification, although other factors may also need to be considered.

The key point to note here is that, early in the risk assessment (and, if you are using a risk assessment tool, early in the tool set-up process), you will need to define your classification guidelines and ensure that asset owners are adequately trained to apply both the guidelines and any related asset labelling scheme developed to meet the requirements of control A.7.2.2 (Information Labelling and Handling).

Are vendors assets?

We identified one of the classes of information assets as '*services* on which computer systems depend: computing and communications services, and general utilities such as heating, lighting, power and air-conditioning'. This gives rise to a simple question: are the suppliers/vendors of these essential services also assets?

There are two practical answers to this question. The best solution is probably to use a mix of the two, but in doing so it is essential that the exact approach to be used in each specific case is determined by a common set of rules. These should be defined in the risk assessment documentation.

One option is to decide that the vendor itself is not an asset – the organisation that is within the scope of the ISMS does not own the vendors – but that the services provided by the vendor and, possibly, the relationship with the vendor are both assets within the scope of the ISMS. The logic behind this option is that a relationship with a vendor can be an asset if it is a key supplier in terms of the information aspects of whatever it is they supply.

For example, a stationery supplier would not, we suggest, be a key relationship for the purposes of information security (even if you argue that without pencils you cannot write, since you can easily go and buy pencils from someone else). On the other hand, if you have invested a lot of time and effort (and hence money) in selecting, educating and building a relationship with a specific supplier, then that relationship has value to you and is therefore, by definition, an asset.

A word of warning however: it is advisable to set clear criteria for inclusion in, or exclusion of suppliers from, the risk assessment process or the process will become unmanageable. So, if it is relatively easy and cost-free to find an alternative provider for any one vendor, without compromise of confidentiality, integrity or availability, then we suggest the relationship is excluded from the asset register. You might like to set some figures for 'relatively easy and cost-free' so that all asset owners apply the criteria consistently when deciding to include/exclude a supplier.

For example, the service provided by a disaster recovery (DR) company is an asset. A contractual relationship with a DR company is part of a control that brings identified risks within an acceptable tolerance, and therefore, of course has value to your company – you pay for it, so it must have.

Vendors, however, bring a whole host of threats with them and these may well provide the context for how you accommodate them in your risk assessment methodology by considering the threat to other assets of them not doing exactly as you might want.

The second approach to vendors is, therefore, to consider them, or rather the danger of them not providing what you require, as a threat. For example, if you have a bespoke piece of software developed by a one-person contractor, the danger is that the one person or source of expertise to service the software becomes unavailable one way or another. This threat could exploit the vulnerability that the software may have e.g. code weaknesses or requires regular maintenance, and you should be able to determine the likelihood of the asset being compromised in this way. The impact is determined by the value of the asset to the business; consequently, the risk can be determined.

What about duplicate copies and backups?

Security breaches in respect of duplicate or backup copies will not necessarily have the same impacts as they would in respect of the originals. Duplicates are usually kept in different media or environments, and are subject to different threats from the originals. The impact on the organisation of compromise in respect of a copy might be the same as, less than or more than the original.

For instance, destruction of a backup copy of an exchange folder will not have the same impact on information availability as would destruction of the original – *unless* the original was already unavailable. Conversely, data confidentiality may be more easily compromised if off-premise backup tapes are attacked than if the servers are threatened. The duplicate copy of an asset must, in other words, be assessed as an asset in its own right.

An alternative approach – more suited to paper copies and digital duplicates of information assets – is to treat the existence of duplicate copies as vulnerabilities in the security of the original asset. The logic is that a photocopy, or an e-copy, will contain all the information that is in the original, but will be beyond the security perimeter devised for the original. The existence of the copy is, therefore, a vulnerability in respect of the original; one logical control is to disable all copying capability.

There is a relevant sub-question in relation to backups, which concerns the security of the various information assets that are backed up to a single source.

Backups should be considered as a specific asset. Backups are kept and generated in order to mitigate a specific risk, but the backups themselves face risks, either the same ones as the original assets they back up and/or different ones, but those risks have to be identified and mitigated. With regards to the ISMS and the information risk assessment you can treat a backup tape (say) as one asset, even though it contains duplicates of many separate assets. This makes sense as any controls applied to the backup will typically be applied to the whole, rather than sub-sections of it. Yes, it contains many assets, all of which have their own classification and impact value, but the challenge of assessing backups of each and every asset separately would be impractical and would add no real value.

The important thing to remember is that when applying controls relating to confidentiality to the individual assets that are backed up, the same degree of restriction should be applied to that part of the backup media on which they are stored – and, where a backup contains assets of varying sensitivity, the classification level appropriate to the most sensitive should be applied to all.

Identification of existing controls

ISO27001 says that the risk assessment must take account of existing controls. This means that you need to identify the controls that are in place at the point you commence your risk assessment. You do this, as ISO27005 points out, to 'avoid unnecessary work or cost, e.g. in the duplication of a control' (8.2.1.4) and recommends that this step should be carried out at the time of identifying the assets. This makes sense; you will find it useful to have to hand information about existing controls as you start considering threats and vulnerabilities. Information about existing controls should be included with the asset information; sensible risk assessment tools will enable you to gather this information in a format that reflects the controls contained in Annex A of ISO27001.

CHAPTER 9: THREATS AND VULNERABILITIES

The second step in the ISO27001 risk assessment process is to identify the threats to the identified assets. The third step is to identify the vulnerabilities those threats might exploit. Threats and vulnerabilities go together and, for that reason, we are addressing them together in this chapter.

The difference between 'threats' and 'vulnerabilities' is not always immediately clear to people new to the subject and, as a risk assessment process is implemented within an organisation, it will not be immediately clear to everyone involved in it. It is very important to always differentiate clearly between these two attributes of a risk, because the existence of the risk itself is dependent on the co-existence of a threat and a vulnerability.

The simple difference is this:

- vulnerabilities are flaws or weaknesses in an asset, whereas,

- threats can accidentally trigger or intentionally exploit a vulnerability to compromise some aspect of the asset.

The first thing to remember is that there are very many threats that have absolutely no relevance to many organisations. A simplistic example would be an organisation that has no Internet connectivity: it can be blithely unconcerned with the huge array of Internet-based threats, because there is no vector that those threats can exploit to attack the network and, therefore, it has no exposure to them.

The moment that it connects to the Internet, it does need to be concerned; the point of connection is by definition a possible point of vulnerability and, therefore, an area where controls might be required. As we shall see later, control selection should depend on the organisation's assessment of the likelihood and potential impact of specific Internet threats and should be focused on trying either to reduce the level of the threat or to reduce the extent of the vulnerability.

Threats, in other words, are external to information assets, and vulnerabilities are typically attributes of the asset – aspects of the asset that the threat can exploit. While threats tend to be external to the assets, they are not necessarily external to the organisation. The majority of information security incidents today originate within the organisation's secure perimeter.

The range of threats includes: hostile outsiders, such as hackers, non-hostile outsiders, such as suppliers or cleaning contractors, and insiders, both the disaffected and the committed, but also the careless or just the poorly trained. Vulnerabilities are security weaknesses in the existing systems, which can either be exploited by threats or which allow damage, accidental or otherwise, to information assets.

For example, dropping a laptop is a threat to the asset (the laptop), and the vulnerability exploited by that could be the lack of robustness in the laptop's design. Similarly, a liquid spillage may be a threat to a laptop and the vulnerability would be its lack of keyboard waterproofing.

For each of the assets within the scope of the ISMS, it is necessary to identify the potential threats and the possible vulnerabilities. The essential relationship, from an information security point of view, between threats and vulnerabilities leads us to think of them as 'combinations'. We're not concerned with either threats or vulnerabilities on their own, but with them in combination. We therefore speak of 'threat-vulnerability combinations'. There are a number of threat-vulnerability combinations that apply to any one asset, and any one threat typically may have more than one vulnerability that it can exploit. It should also be noted that a threat to one asset is not necessarily a threat to another. For example, a fire in the server room is a threat to a number of systems based there, but is unlikely to be a threat to an organisation's externally-hosted mobile phone network.

There are very many threats and the range of possible vulnerabilities is also substantial. Examples of threats and vulnerabilities are contained in ISO27005, BS7799-3 and NIST SP 800-30. Whilst threat and vulnerability databases are not widely available, any good risk assessment tool should contain both.

Some threat-vulnerability combinations will be unique to specific industries, which may lead to the introduction of controls additional to those in ISO27001 Annex A. Many of the threats and their related vulnerabilities will also be technical in nature. Technical vulnerabilities need special treatment, and these are further discussed below.

The requirements of the standard are as follows:

Threats

As we've said, threats[45] are things that can go wrong or that can 'attack' the identified assets. They can be either external or internal. Examples might include fire or fraud, virus or worm, hacker or terrorist. Threats are always present for every system or asset – because it is valuable to its owner, it will be valuable to someone else. You could assume that, if you cannot identify a threat to an asset, that it is not really an asset. So the next stage, mandated by ISO27001, is to identify the potential threats to the systems and assets listed in compliance with A.7.1.1, and identified in the previous chapter.

Essentially, threats for each of the systems should be considered under the headings of:

• threats to confidentiality,

• threats to integrity, and

• threats to availability.

Some threats will fall under one heading only, others under more than one. It is important to have carried out this analysis systematically and comprehensively, to ensure that no threats are ignored or missed. The quality of the controls that the organisation eventually implements will reflect the quality of this exercise, and of the overall risk assessment.

A number of external threats might be classified under all three headings. A hacker might be able to steal confidential data and then disrupt the information system so that data is no longer available or, if it is, it is corrupted. A virus can not only affect the integrity and availability of data but also,

---

[45] ISO27001 clause 4.2.1 - d2.

because it could mail out a copy of an address book, confidentiality as well. A business interruption, such as a fire in the server room, or a filing cabinet, is initially likely to affect the availability and integrity of information.

Identify, on an individual basis, threats to the confidentiality, integrity and availability of every asset within the scope of the ISMS. You can do this through a brainstorming exercise or by using an appropriate threat database; technical expertise is essential if the threat identification step is to be carried out properly.

It is, as we've said, likely that an individual threat may appear against a number of assets but, crucially, ISO27001 requires the ISMS to be erected on the foundation of a detailed identification and assessment of the threats to each individual information asset that is within the scope. From a practical point of view, if a number of assets fall within the same class and are exactly the same (e.g. desktop computers that have the same hardware specifications, software build, connectivity configuration and user exposure) they might be considered a group of assets and the subsequent phases of this exercise could be carried out treating them on that basis. Where there is any doubt or uncertainty, however, resort to assessing threats on an individual asset basis.

Vulnerabilities

Vulnerabilities[46] leave a system open to attack by something that is classified as a threat, or allow an attack to have some success or greater impact. For example, for the

---

[46] ISO27001 clause 4.2.1 - d3.

external threat of 'fire', a vulnerability could be the presence of inflammable materials (e.g. paper) in the server room. In the language of ISO27001, a vulnerability can be exploited by a threat.

The next stage in the assessment process, therefore, is to identify – for every single one of the assets that you have identified and for each of the threats that you have listed alongside each of the assets – the vulnerabilities that each threat could exploit. Clearly, a single asset could face a number of threats, and each threat could exploit more than one vulnerability.

A common question is: Should we identify vulnerabilities with or without those controls that are currently in place? Does the fact, for instance, that we have a firewall mean that we do not have a vulnerability to hacking attacks?

The correct answer is that you should do both. You should identify the vulnerability that would be exploited by the threat if you didn't have any controls in place, because you want to assure yourself that those controls which are in place are appropriate for the identified risks (in some cases, implemented controls are in excess of those identified as actually required in the light of the assessed risks and the organisation's risk appetite). You also want to identify the controls that are currently in place, and you want to be in a position to identify any residual risk (*see Chapter 13*), in order to consider whether or not additional controls may be required. Those controls that are already in place will be operated as part of the organisation's ISMS and the confirmation that they are appropriate controls, and are to be retained, must come from the formal risk assessment.

Technical vulnerabilities

Many of the threats related to information technology arise because of technical vulnerabilities. A number of information systems are sold with in-built and widely known vulnerabilities. All wireless (WiFi) products, for example, are designed to communicate 'out of the box' with one another and, therefore, come without any security settings configured. Routers and other access control units come with default password settings that are widely known. All software has imperfections, and the more complex the software, the more imperfections it will have. Each imperfection is a potential vulnerability. CVE[47] identifies in excess of 23,000 unique, standardised names of vulnerabilities and security weaknesses. Bugtraq[48] has over 700 pages listing publicly-known software vulnerabilities, across all operating systems and applications.

Attacks are often devised to exploit specific vulnerabilities.[49] An increasing number of attacks are made before patches are available, and exploit code for many of the most popular attacks is commonly available on the Internet. Many attacks are automated and indiscriminate (geographically, sectorally and size-wise) in their target selection. Integrity and availability of data are, often, more likely to be compromised by these threat-vulnerability combinations than is confidentiality. The SANS *Top Cyber*

---

[47] CVE, the Common Vulnerabilities and Exposures dictionary, is at *http://cve.mitre.org*.
[48] Bugtraq is at *www.securityfocus.com/vulnerabilities*.
[49] There is a description, in Chapter 13 of *IT Governance: A Manager's Guide to Data Security and ISO 27001/ISO 27002*, Alan Calder and Steve G Watkins (Kogan Page, 2007), of malware; Chapter 18 of that book deals with hackers and their various motivations.

Security Risks[50] is a list of the most popular current attacks on information systems.

Your risk assessment should not, however, attempt to individually identify every single one of these threat-vulnerability combinations. There are too many of them. New ones are constantly appearing while old ones continuously evolve. What you *should* do is identify the generic threat (hacking, malicious code or malware) and the generic vulnerability (software weaknesses), with a generically high likelihood and a medium or high impact.

The control that you would apply is the generic control A.12.6.1 (Control of Technical Vulnerabilities). The baseline implementation of this control should be to ensure that all vulnerabilities identified in the SANS *Top Cyber Security Risks* are secured. Thereafter, appropriate external vulnerability or penetration tests should be run on a regular basis (weekly, monthly or quarterly – depending on your risk assessment), to identify whether or not newly identified vulnerabilities have appeared in the software deployed on your network, and these should be patched to a priority determined by their potential risk.

Today's combination attacks, and the growing usage of Trojans and key loggers, suggests that external vulnerability testing should be combined with some form of software scanning, this side of your secure perimeter, to discover whether or not any malware that has the potential to open your network to the outside has installed itself on the inside.

A.12.6.1

---

[50] Published by the SANS Institute, at *www.sans.org/top-cyber-security-risks*

CHAPTER 10: IMPACT AND ASSET VALUATION

The successful exploitation of a vulnerability by a threat will have an impact on the asset's availability, confidentiality or integrity. This may have consequences for the business, in terms of its actual operations, or from a compliance angle, or in relation to a contractual requirement. A single threat could exploit more than one vulnerability and each exploitation could have more than one type of impact. These impacts should all be identified.

Risk assessment involves identifying the potential business harm that might result from each of these identified impacts. The way to do this is to assess the extent of the possible loss to the business for each potential impact. One object of this exercise is to prioritise treatment (controls) and to do so in the context of the organisation's acceptable risk threshold, so it makes sense to categorise possible loss in terms of impact on the organisation of losing the identified asset attribute.

Impacts

6.1.2©0

Clause 4.2.1 - d4 of ISO27001 requires that the organisation 'analyzes the impacts that losses of confidentiality, integrity and availability may have on each of the assets'. ISO27001 also requires the organisation to 'develop criteria for accepting risks and identify the acceptable levels of risk' (4.2.1 - c2). It provides *no* 6.1.2(a) *guidance* as to how those criteria should be developed other (b) than suggesting (in 4.2.1 - e1) that they should be based on the 'business impacts upon the organization that might 6.1.2(d)(e) result from security failures, taking into account the consequences of a loss of confidentiality, integrity or availability of the assets'.

Furthermore, ISO27001 provides *no guidance* as to the basis on which control selection decisions should be made, other than to say that the 'selection shall take account of the criteria for accepting risks as well as legal, regulatory and contractual requirements' (4.2.1 - g).

Finally, ISO27001 has *no requirement* in terms of your methodology for the valuation of information assets.

How you value an asset is, however, going to be fundamental to how much you will be prepared to invest in protecting it. ISO27001 simply defines an asset as 'anything that has value to the organization' (clause 3.1), but does not specify how that value should be assessed. The organisation's fixed asset register is unlikely to provide practical help in this regard: many critical assets may already (through application of the financial depreciation policy, or of the accounting convention that assets should be shown on the balance sheet at the *lower* of historic cost – less depreciation – or current market value) have been written down below their actual useful value to the organisation. Many other, even more critical, assets (such as brand value, key supplier and customer contracts, staff know-how, intellectual property and databases) may not even be on the fixed asset register at all. Many of these assets may even have a current market value in excess of the historic cost and, in some cases, this value appreciates over time, rather than depreciates.

Resolution of these issues is fundamental to the development of an ISMS that will meet the requirements of ISO27001; you must have clearly defined criteria that enable management to 'knowingly and objectively' accept risks (4.2.1 - f2). These criteria must reflect some practical 6,1,3(d) relationship between the potential impact of an information asset-related threat on the organisation and the level of investment that will be made to prevent that happening.

These issues are, therefore, fundamental components of the organisation's risk assessment methodology. As we said earlier, the standard requires the organisation to identify threats to its information assets, the vulnerabilities that might be exploited by those threats, and the impacts that losses of confidentiality, integrity and availability might have on each of those assets.

Furthermore, the results of the risk assessment must be used to inform the correct ascription of controls to assets in light of the value of each asset (i.e. the importance of the asset to the organisation, or the impact on the organisation that would result from a compromise of each of confidentiality, integrity and availability) and the threats and vulnerabilities which, in combination, make up the likelihood of the asset being compromised.

The standard is clear that impacts have to be considered separately for each of confidentiality, availability and integrity, and in each of the business, legal/regulatory and contractual contexts. This is logical because you are likely to select different controls to preserve confidentiality (e.g. encryption) than to ensure availability (e.g. backups). In other words, for any given asset and a specified threat-vulnerability combination (and we will look in more detail at these in the next chapter), you will need to identify the impact on the organisation of a loss of confidentiality, a loss of integrity and a loss of availability.

Defining impact

BS7799-3 recommends (and ISO27005 concurs) that impact 'values should be identified that express the potential business impacts if the confidentiality, integrity or availability, or any other important property of the asset is damaged' (clause 5.4). ISO27001 is concerned specifically with negative impacts, to be described in terms of loss or degradation of the confidentiality, integrity or availability of an asset.

Confidentiality is lost when information suffers unauthorised disclosure. 'Unauthorised' ranges from breach of data protection or privacy legislation, through breach of contractual requirements, to betrayal of commercially or personally sensitive data.

Integrity is lost when unauthorised changes are made to information or information assets, whether accidentally or deliberately. Failure to repair losses of integrity can lead to further corruption and integrity loss in other information assets.

Availability is undermined when those (people or systems) authorised to access information in order to do their jobs are unable to do so.

This means that each asset should have a separate impact assessment for each of confidentiality, integrity and availability. You should, therefore, identify one-by-one, the likely impacts for each threat-vulnerability combination that you identify for each and every asset within the scope of your ISMS, and for each of confidentiality, integrity and availability.

This has to be taken further. Every information asset is, as we have seen, likely to be affected by at least one threat-vulnerability combination. Every such combination might compromise each of the confidentiality, availability and integrity of the asset, which means that you may have to make three yes/no decisions. For each of the three information attributes, there may be an impact that has business consequences, one that has legal/regulatory consequences, and one that has contractual consequences. You must therefore assess, for each of these possibilities, what that impact might be. You have, in other words, potentially nine decision points in respect of each threat-vulnerability combination for each information asset.

Here's an example:

Imagine the risk assessment carried out in relation to an organisation's unencrypted backup tape, and specifically how it is transported to secure off-site storage. A threat – driver forgetfulness or inattention – might exploit a vulnerability – the van door doesn't close properly unless it is forced shut and locked – with the consequence that the backup tape might fall out into the road while in transit. There is a realistic likelihood of this happening, and the potential impacts can be assessed as follows:

Confidentiality of the information on the backup tape will be compromised; the business's reputation for protecting its customer data will be undermined and it will lose a quantifiable level of revenue; there will be legal consequences, which can also be quantified, arising from the breach of the privacy of the individuals whose data is on the tape; and there will be contractual consequences arising from the breach in specific customer contracts that require protection of their data.

Availability of the backup tape will be compromised; the business impact may be an inability to continue operations when faced with a business continuity event and this will have quantifiable consequences; the legal consequence may be that the directors are prosecuted for their failure to be adequately prepared to protect the company's assets; the contractual consequences may include a breach of a customer contractual requirement for effective backup processes.

Integrity of the backup tape may be compromised because the tape may be damaged on falling out of the van while it is in transit; this will have a business impact when it proves impossible to restore the most recent version of a specific user document that has been corrupted in error; it may have a legal consequence when a later court case is unable to access a critical document for which no other copies exist; and it may have contractual consequences if the tape contains data that has to be surrendered to the customer on completion of the contract.

Whilst methodologies do exist that, having determined individual values for these impacts, then add or multiply them together to try to reduce the actual risk assessment workload, practical experience demonstrates that the results produced by these methodologies skew the risk treatment decisions. For instance, an asset with a very high confidentiality impact level and a very low availability impact level needs different controls for risks to confidentiality than to availability. Should you apply controls that are more appropriate for one risk than the other, or should you apply something 'in the middle' that is appropriate for neither? In either case, what you have is a situation in which your risk treatment decision is not directly related to the risk, and the investment in the controls is unlikely to be in proportion to the potential impact against which you are guarding. In other words, this sort of approach is unlikely to lead either to an ISMS that conforms to ISO27001 or to one that is cost-effectively optimised.

The risk analysis above doesn't yet include an assessment as to the actual cost of the impact on the organisation in any of the nine identified areas, nor does it include an assessment as to the likelihood of occurrence of the threat-vulnerability combination, and it is, therefore, impossible to determine which of the identified risks should be accepted, which rejected and which transferred or controlled.

Estimating impact

Part of how we make that decision has to take into account the cost of controlling the risk: should we spend more, less than, or the same as, the potential cost of the impact on controlling the risk?

ISO27001 defines the purpose of an ISMS as 'ensuring the selection of adequate and proportionate security controls that protect information assets and give confidence to interested parties' (clause 1.1). ISO27002 goes further. It says:

Expenditure on controls needs to be balanced against the business harm likely to result from business failures. [clause 0.4]

Risk assessment should include the systematic approach of estimating the magnitude of risks (risk analysis) and the process of comparing the estimated risks against risk criteria to determine the significance of the risks (risk evaluation). [clause 4.1]

This is helpful guidance, in that it talks about 'estimating magnitude', not 'quantifying cost', of risks, and about 'proportionate' security controls. This guidance, which is in line with a qualitative risk assessment methodology, is a particularly helpful starting point for considering impact value.

BS7799-3 takes this guidance further: it says that assets should be valued to take 'account of the identified legal and business requirements and the impacts resulting from a loss of confidentiality, integrity and availability' (clause 5.1). It goes on to suggest that 'one way to express asset values is to use the business impacts that unwanted incidents, such as disclosure, modification, non-availability and/or destruction, would have to the asset and the related business interests that would be directly or indirectly damaged' (clause 5.4). The value of the asset should, in simple terms, be the same as the impact value of compromising it. ISO27005, in talking (at clause 8.2.1.6) about the 'business consequences if [the assets] are damaged or compromised', is taking the same view as BS7799-3.

Our earlier analysis of the threat-vulnerability combinations that might compromise a backup tape is in line with the view that assets should have more than one value. BS7799-3 confirms this view: 'values should be identified that express the potential business impacts if the confidentiality, integrity or availability, or any other important property of the asset is damaged' (clause 5.4) and suggests that a standard asset valuation scale should be defined for assets to assist asset owners in correctly valuing their assets.

BS7799-3 recommends the creation of an asset impact valuation scale to guide asset owners in their valuation activity. The starting point for the creation of such a scale is to estimate the possible cost of impact. One traditional method (one that we recommend, and which is also contained in ISO27005) of estimating impact is to identify, value and aggregate all the direct (e.g. legal) and indirect (e.g. brand diminution) costs of an event, all the costs of recovery, repair, rectification and (possibly) lost opportunities and lost revenue. The resulting total cost of (potential) loss is the impact value.

A stepped set of impact levels (e.g. high-medium-low) can then be designed that reflects the ranges of estimated impact, such that, for instance, all impacts with an estimated cost between £15k and £150k might be classified as 'medium'. These levels should be appropriate to the size of the organisation, its appetite for risk and its current risk treatment framework. They should be approved by management, as part of their approval of the overall risk management framework.

While it is true that, in reality, there will be variations between the actual impact of different threat-vulnerability combinations, there is no value in calculating these variations precisely: the range within which the impact value of similar threat-vulnerability combinations might fall is such that the same control decisions are likely to be made in respect of each. A qualitative methodology, which enables you to look at similar risk levels as though they were the same, is cost-effective and produces comparable and reproducible results.

You should note that, although you are using monetary values to make the boundary levels comprehensible to assessors, the reason for this is to ensure that they are able to produce comparable results, rather than to apply a quantitative methodology, which this is not.

Your risk assessment approach should, therefore, ask you to input impact values separately for each of confidentiality, integrity and availability. More than that, it should follow BS7799-3 and or ISO27005 and the methodology we outline here. Use impact values as the asset values.

The starting point in asset impact assessment is to identify the 'owner' (as described in ISO/IEC 27001:2005, 4.2.1 - d1 footnote), the person who decides how the asset is used, by whom and for what purpose. The owner is best placed to explain and evaluate the damage done to the organisation if the asset's confidentiality, integrity or availability is compromised. The asset owner should consider what business processes the asset supports, as well as the legal and contractual requirements in terms of the asset, and derive from these the value of the asset in terms of the cost to the organisation of compromise to each of the asset's three information security attributes: confidentiality, integrity and availability.

When valuing each asset, the key question is: What value does this attribute of this asset have to the organisation and what would it cost us if it were compromised? The fixed asset register valuation and the financial cost of replacement are at best likely to be minor contributors to this exercise, which is far more based on a qualitative assessment of value.

The scale of this exercise is substantial. It is extremely difficult to carry out manually, requiring an excessive commitment of resources. It may also involve an assessment methodology that contains a high level of subjectivity, as a result of which the methodology is likely to fall foul of the 'comparable and reproducible' requirement. The only way that the risk assessment can be done cost-effectively, in terms of resource deployment and process accuracy, is by using an appropriate risk assessment tool.

The asset valuation table

We've said that the organisation would find an asset valuation table useful to guide risk assessors in assigning values to information assets within the scope of the ISMS. We have already seen that the risk assessment needs to produce reproducible and comparable results, and consistency in asset valuation is essential to this.

We also summed up current guidance on the approach to asset valuation by pointing to BS7799-3 guidance which says that assets should be valued to take 'account of the identified legal and business requirements and the impacts resulting from a loss of confidentiality, integrity and availability' (clause 5.1) and that 'one way to express asset values is to use the business impacts that unwanted incidents, such as disclosure, modification, non-availability and/or destruction, would have to the asset and the related business interests that would be directly or indirectly damaged' (clause 5.4). Clearly, the asset value is not the original cost of acquisition, nor is it the cost of replacement – although these aspects should be included in the impact valuation.

In a qualitative methodology, we need an appropriate asset valuation scale to support this process. You could use the following table:

Asset: Value → ↓ Security Attribute	Low	Medium	High
Confidentiality	Impact is less than £15k	Impact £15k – £149k	Impact in excess of £150k
Integrity	Impact is less than £15k	Impact £15k – £149k	Impact in excess of £150k
Availability	Impact is less than £15k	Impact £15k – £149k	Impact in excess of £150k

Figure 10: Asset valuation table

In this table, the impact in each instance is the total cost of impact, including reputation damage, which itself is briefly discussed later in this chapter.

The impact evaluation should include, as part of this total cost of loss:

- monetary loss;

- productivity loss (which relates to the role of the asset in business processes);

- loss of customer confidence; and

- reputation damage.

It also needs to take into account:

- objective(s) of process(es);

- criticality of process(es) to the business and business objectives; and

- information sensitivity.

Business, legal and contractual impact values

In your risk assessment methodology, it is permissible to use, as the impact value, the highest of confidentiality, integrity and availability values, or a sum of them, or to carry out the assessment separately for each attribute of each asset. The third is usually the most sensible approach to pursue, as many controls are designed to deal with security issues around one – but not all – of the three information security attributes.

You should also remember that ISO27001 requires the risk assessment to take into account the business, legal or regulatory and contractual requirements for information security; it is entirely possible that, in respect of an individual asset, there will be different requirements and, therefore, different values in each of these areas.

For instance, a police force must keep personal data confidential so that it can comply with the Data Protection Act, but it may also need to ensure that the information is available to other police forces investigating a crime (business need). A healthcare provider will have a contractual responsibility to keep patient information confidential, a business requirement to maintain the integrity of that information (for instance, keeping the medical history up to date) and a compliance requirement to protect that data from exposure. The potential impacts of a breach of security in each of these areas could be different.

You, therefore, have to consider how the information is actually used in the organisation – in other words, in the context of the business, legal and regulatory and contractual requirements for information security – before you can really make an informed decision about the most appropriate approach to pursue.

This means that, for every information asset, you will have three contexts in which to carry out a risk assessment – business, legal/regulatory and contractual. In each context, you will need to assess impacts to confidentiality, integrity and availability. There are, potentially, therefore, nine assessments to make in respect of each asset. It is likely, for every asset, that one or more of these nine attributes will have little or no value, and that the impact in relation to one will be the same as in relation to another. While these are all acceptable inputs to the risk assessment, it will still be logical to start with this detailed approach. In any case, your methodology must be sufficiently practical to actually work, and a fully ISO27001-compliant risk assessment tool should automate and simplify risk assessments being made for each information security attribute for each of business, legal and contractual requirements.

Reputation damage

Reputation damage – a major concern of boardrooms and shareholders – is likely to be an impact of most breaches of information security. It can, however, be very hard to incorporate into a risk assessment process where the results need to be 'comparable and reproducible'.

Again, the solution for this challenge can be as simple or as complicated as you want to make it. We recommend using one of the two following approaches:

Direct description approach

The direct approach is one where the asset owners use an agreed customisation of the table which follows (Figure 11), to determine the contribution that reputation damage would have on the impact value for that (attribute or component of that) asset for risk assessment purposes.

Coverage approach

An alternative approach, in which the contribution of reputation damage to the value of the asset is estimated in light of the adverse coverage that might result, could use a customised version of the table on page 127 (Figure 12).

Each entry in the level of impact column would be given a value and this would be used in helping to determine which impact band in Figure 10 the value of the asset falls into.

Of course, those organisations that do not have a reputation to protect will not need to factor in this aspect of impact; for those that do, the input of the organisation's PR advisers may be particularly useful.

Description of impact of reputation damage	Contribution to impact value of asset
Likely to jeopardise existence of organisation	£££££££££££££ £££££££££££££
Likely to jeopardise ability to function in one sector and/or geographical area (continent or country)	££££££ ££££££
Likely to result in law suit directly related to core competence	££££
Likely to result in law suit not directly related to core competence	££
Likely to jeopardise relationship with one or more existing high-worth clients	££
Likely to create ill feeling in one or more high-worth clients	£
Likely to jeopardise relationship with five or more low-worth clients	¾ £
Likely to create ill-feeling with more than one low-worth client	½ £
Likely to create ill-feeling with one low-worth client	¼ £

Figure 11: Direct impact of reputation damage

Contribution to impact value of asset	Media coverage			Specific client level
	TV	Press	Radio	
£££££££££££££££££	National	National	National	-
£££££££££££££££	Regional	National	National	-
£££££££££££££££	Regional	Regional	National	-
££££££££££	-	National	Regional	-
££££££££	-	Local	Regional	-
££££££	-	Local	Local	-
££££	-	-	Local	-
££££££££	-	-	-	Jeopardise reputation with one sector
££££	-	-	-	Damage reputation with one major client that jeopardises current and future contracts
££	-	-	-	Damage reputation with one major client that jeopardises future contracts

Figure 12: Coverage impact of reputation damage

CHAPTER 11: LIKELIHOOD

Each of the preceding stages of the risk assessment has a relatively high degree of certainty about it. The vulnerabilities should be capable of technical, logical or physical identification. The way in which threats might exploit them should also be mechanically demonstrable. The decisions that have to be made are those that relate to the actions the organisation will take to counter those threats. Before that, however, there needs to be an assessment as to the likelihood of the event, and what the appropriate response to it will be. This means that the actual risks have now to be assessed and related to the organisation's overall 'risk appetite' – that is, its willingness to take risks.

Risk analysis

ISO27001 (clause 4.2.1 – e) sets out the requirements in terms of analysing the risks. Until this point, the assessment has been carried out as though there was an equal likelihood of every identified threat actually happening. This is not really the case and this is, therefore, where there must be an assessment – for every identified impact – of the likelihood or probability of it actually occurring. 'Likelihood' in the risk equation is a value representing the probability of an identified threat exploiting a specific vulnerability in the asset.

Probabilities might range from 'not very likely' (e.g. major earthquake in Southern England destroying primary and backup facilities) to 'almost daily' (e.g. several hundred automated malware and hack attacks against the network). Again, a simple set of stepped, qualitative levels should be used.

The likelihood level should be estimated by considering the frequency at which the threat is likely to occur in the future and the probability of the threat exploiting and/or breaching the vulnerability when it does occur:

Likelihood = Frequency of threat occurring x Probability of vulnerability being breached

Most methodologies simply make, for each identified threat, a single assessment as to the likelihood of the threat occurring and exploiting the vulnerability, and then mapping that level directly to the estimated impact level in order to arrive at an assessed risk level.

Some methodologies insert an intermediate step, which involves a matrix that helps calculate the likelihood level by reference to the probability of both the threat occurring and the probability of it successfully exploiting the identified vulnerability.

For example, an intermediate likelihood matrix constructed on that basis might look like the one in Figure 13, opposite.

In this example, using three-level scales for each of the vulnerability and threat frequency axes gives a five-level (very low – low – medium – high – very high) likelihood scale. Of course, the boundaries for each of the scales for the threat and vulnerability axes need to be defined so that the assessment results can be reproduced and will be comparable.

	High	Medium	High	Very high
Probability of vulnerability breach	Medium	Low	Medium	High
	Low	Very low	Low	Medium
		Low	Medium	High

Figure 13: Likelihood matrix

Frequency of threat occurrence

Either approach is acceptable for the ISO27001 risk assessment. As long as the method for determination of likelihood is defined so that it can be estimated in a manner by which it is reproducible and comparable the process will satisfy the requirements of the standard. The decision as to whether or not there should be an intermediate step is one entirely for the organisation.

Information to support assessments

For the risk assessment methodology to provide 'reproducible and comparable results', there certainly needs to be some objective basis of guidance for assessing or estimating likelihood.

A key challenge is that, while risk assessment may draw substantially on historic records, risk management decisions are based primarily on assessments of the future. Whilst one can – and should – use history (and that means collecting, analysing and improving detailed monitoring statistics) in order to inform one's assessment of the future, it is extremely important to bear in mind that 'things change' and the 'thing' that changes most for today's organisations is the risk environment.

Just because a threat has never occurred to date does not mean that it never will. This may seem an obvious statement, but it is the implications of it that need to be kept in mind when conducting and reviewing risk assessments. The rate of change in technology alone is, for instance, a key source of risk for enterprises.

Historic data, facts and figures are all, nevertheless, going to be of enormous value in the risk management process. Historic figures about the risk environment (frequency and nature of threats, the cost of successful attacks, the costs of various mitigation measures, and so on) all inform the initial risk assessment, as well as the ongoing risk management process. As we shall see in due course, ISO27001 expects us to measure the effectiveness of the controls that we select and to use this information to feed the continuous improvement process.

There are a number of challenges in creating this data, including:

- defining a robust methodology, one that enables the process and outcome to be reproducible and comparable, for estimating costs, such as reputational damage, the inadvertent disclosure of confidential information, and disaster recovery costs;

- evaluating control implementation costs, and particularly their impact on productivity;

- the rate of change in threats, technology/vulnerabilities and control options/tools to address them; and

- ascribing values and likelihoods to potential future events, in an environment which is more likely to bring new threats than to repeat old ones.

It will be essential that the risk management process has built into it sub-processes for collecting relevant information about threats and activities undertaken and, particularly, about changes in the risk environment, so that management can use this information to improve and strengthen its information security management system.

CHAPTER 12: RISK LEVEL

Risk level – the output of the risk equation that we discussed earlier – is a function of impact and likelihood (probability). The final step in the risk assessment exercise is to assess the risk level for each impact and to transfer the details to the corporate asset inventory.

Three levels of risk assessment are usually adequate: low, medium and high. Where the likely impact is low and the probability is also low, then the risk level could be considered very low. Where the impact is at least high and the probability is also at least high, then the risk level might (depending on the design of the risk matrix) be either high or very high.

Every organisation has to decide for itself what it wants to set as the thresholds for categorising each potential impact and from time to time it may be helpful to have four or more risk levels (including one such as minimal) in order to better prioritise actions.

The risk scale

The basic risk scale, which is set out overleaf, plots estimated impact against estimated likelihood.

In this scale, a different category of labels has been applied to both the impact (lower case alphabetic characters) and the likelihood (lower case Roman numerals) scales to indicate low, medium and high. The reason for doing this is to avoid confusion in discussions and communications between members of the risk assessment team and with

12: Risk Level

other parties. For example, a high likelihood (iii) and a high impact (c) identify something that would be very high risk, whereas a medium risk in the table is a function of likelihood (i) and impact (c), or (ii) and (b), or (iii) and (a).

High			
c	Medium	High	Very high
b	Low	Medium	High
a	Very low	Low	Medium
	i	ii	iii

Impact

Likelihood

Low   High

Figure 14: The risk scale

While that is clear, the table only becomes useful when each band has objective criteria applied to it which enable different people in different parts of the organisation to use it on a consistent basis.

The usual way of doing this is to allocate specific ranges to each band. For instance, the impact bands might be:

Impact

c   From £1m to £5m (anything in excess of £5m is rejected)

b   From £100,000 to £999,999

a   From zero to £99,999.

The likelihood bands might be:

Likelihood

i   Less than once every year (very infrequent)

ii   Between once a month and once a year (often)

iii   More than once a month (very often).

These bands enable different people, in different parts of the organisation, to assess risks in a similar way. Automated hacking attacks on an online bank, for instance, would be placed in impact category b (between £100,000 and £999,999) and likelihood category iii (very often); the assessed risk level would therefore be 'high'. Similarly, manual hack attacks might be placed in impact level c (over £1m) but only at likelihood level ii (often). Intersection of these two lines would also give rise to an assessed risk of 'high'.

The qualitative methodology has been useful in enabling different threat-vulnerability combinations to be quickly assessed, and for comparative risk assessment decisions to be made – without detailed, faux-accurate calculations as to potential impact.

Both risks fall outside the organisation's risk tolerance level, and both should be controlled. The organisation's risk acceptance criteria include the requirement that the cost of control should be in line with the identified potential impact. But how do we determine, in this example, how much to spend on implementation?

Boundary calculations

One approach is to calculate the risk value (risk = impact x likelihood) at the borders of each risk value and for the investment criteria to be as simple as: spend no less than [the lower risk level] and no more than [the higher risk level]. Each level has an upper and a lower boundary, the point at which the risk shifts from being at one level to being at the next. For example, the border values for 'very low' in our table would be:

Lower boundary: a (low) x i (low), or 0 x 0, which equals zero.

Upper boundary: a (high) x i (high), or 1 x £99,999, which equals £99,999.

In other words, according to this risk assessment scale, this risk would have an impact that falls somewhere between £0 and £99,999 and the risk treatment decision (if this risk was outside the risk acceptance boundary) would allow no more than £99,999 to be invested in control implementation.

While this appears clear cut, the situation is less clear for those risk levels that occur more than once. For instance, the medium risk level (let's call it risk 1 in this example) could fall within the ranges of:

Impact high (c) and likelihood low (i), the boundaries of which would be:

Lower boundary: c (low) x i (low), or £1m x 0, which equals 0.

Upper boundary: c (high) x i (high), or £5m x 1, which equals £5m.

The medium risk level also exists at the intersection of impact (b) and likelihood (ii). The boundary calculations (for what we will call risk 2 in this example) would be:

Lower boundary: b (low) x ii (low), or £100,000 x 1, which is £100,000.

Upper boundary: b (high) x ii (high), or £999,999 x 12, which is (about) £12m.

So, a risk (Risk 1), assessed as a medium risk, has a potential impact of between £0 and £5m. Another risk (Risk 2), also assessed as a medium risk, has a potential impact of between £100,000 and £12m. These clearly different impact ranges need to be recognised when developing the organisational risk assessment methodology, and there are three useful ways of responding to them.

- The first is to ensure that the scale you use is sufficiently granular; in real terms, a five-level scale may – for many organisations – provide a more useful basis of assessment.

- The second is for the risk assessment methodology to explicitly recognise that there will be 'fuzzy areas' at the boundaries, and for the board to delegate authority to the risk assessor to review and adjust (what we call 'smoothing') those individual control decisions that appear to be misaligned as a result of these calculations, to ensure that there is an equivalence of investment.

- The third is to use 'mid-points' instead of boundary calculations to provide guidance on control investment. While these calculations do not remove the need to address both points 1 and 2 above, they do reduce the magnitude of the overlap and, therefore, can provide more useful risk assessment guidance.

Mid-point calculations

An alternative, and more helpful, approach is to calculate the mid-points for each range, and to use those calculated numbers to guide investment decisions.

The starting point for this calculation is to identify mid-points (i.e. the points between the upper and lower levels) for each of the risk factors (likelihood and impact). The mid-points for each of the factors in Figure 14, above, would be:

Ic	=	£5m	Li	=	0.5 (times a year)
Ib	=	£500,000	Lii	=	6 (times a year)
Ia	=	£50,000	Liii	=	52 (times a year)

We can then apply these to calculate the mid-point for each of the identified risks, to produce what we call a 'risk value indicator'. Please note the term 'indicator': we are using a qualitative methodology, and this is an indicator to provide guidance.

12: Risk Level

Risk level				Risk value indicator	
Very high	=	Liii x Ic	= 52 x £2.5m	= £130m/yr
High	=	Liii x Ib	= 52 x £500k	= £26m/yr
	=	Lii x Ic	= 6 x £5m	= £30m/yr
Medium	=	Liii x Ia	= 52 x £50k	= £2.6m/yr
	=	Lii x Ib	= 6 x £500k	= £3.0m/yr
	=	Li x Ic	= 0.5 x £5m	= £2.5m/yr
Low	=	Lii x Ia	= 6 x £50k	= £300k/yr
	=	Li x Ib	= 0.5 x £500k	= £250k/yr
Very low	=	Li x Ia	= 0.5 x £50k	= £25k/yr

As these calculations demonstrate, there is a range of risk value indicators for each risk level, even when considering only the mid-point in the corresponding likelihood and impact scales. From an investment perspective, the control investment decision will be to invest an amount approximately the same as the risk value indicator. As guidance goes, the risk assessment team will find this more useful than guidance which is based on boundary calculations. It is well worth remembering here the 'approximately correct rather than precisely wrong' mantra.

The organisation's documented risk acceptance criteria should, if a mid-point calculation is used, include a description of how it is calculated and how the risk value indicator is to be used in risk treatment decisions. The formal risk acceptance criteria should also state that, while it is the mid-points that have been used to demonstrate the different levels of risk and guide control investment decisions, it is the entire level that is either within or outside the acceptance criteria.

CHAPTER 13: RISK TREATMENT AND THE SELECTION OF CONTROLS

Once you have completed the risk assessment, you can move on to the selection of controls, and this chapter reviews the requirements of ISO27001 around control selection, which is also known as 'risk treatment'.

As we said in Chapter 1, there are four risk treatment decisions that can be made:

- accept the risk;

- eliminate the risk by work-around or other arrangements;

- control the risk to bring it to an acceptable level;

- transfer it to a third party (e.g. via insurance).

The criterion that is used in making the decision is simple: either the risk is within the risk tolerance level, in which case it is accepted, or it is not, in which case it must be avoided, controlled or transferred. So, in principle (unless the risk is too great), if:

- Risk level < risk acceptance criteria, then 'accept risk' or, if,

- Risk level > risk acceptance criteria, then 'treat' risk.

If the risk is too great (i.e. the potential impact is off the scale, or is greater than the 'very high' level chosen in the risk assessment methodology), then the risk must be avoided, which might involve implementing some form of 'work-around' in order to do so. A simple example of this response to a risk assessment might be where the potential impact of theft of equipment from the offices of a company would be so great if it moved to a particular neighbourhood that it decided against the move.

Types of controls

Controls (4.2.1 - f) are the countermeasures or safeguards designed to reduce risks, and are applied to reduce the likelihood of something happening or of its impact, if it were to happen. There are three types of control that are commonly applied to reduce the risk:

- Preventive controls protect vulnerabilities and make an attack unsuccessful or reduce its impact.

- Corrective controls reduce the impact of an attack and/or help with recovery after an attack.

- Detective controls discover attacks and trigger preventive or corrective controls.

Control types can fall into three different categories:

- Technical controls, which usually involve system, hardware or software packages, measures and configurations and deal with, for example, identity, cryptography and security administration:
  - prevent
  - detect
  - correct (or recover).

- Management controls, which relate to direction, guidelines, policies and procedures put in place by management:
  - prevent
  - detect

- correct (recover).

- Operational controls, those controls that deal with day-to-day issues such as backups, physical security and so on:

  - prevent
  - detect
  - correct (recover).

As we indicated in Chapter 3, it is essential that the controls that are implemented are cost-effective. The principle is that the cost of implementing and maintaining a control should be no greater than the cost of the impact at the identified frequency, and this principle should be written into the board-approved risk acceptance criteria contained in the information security policy.

There are also practical considerations that should be borne in mind when selecting controls:

- likely effectiveness of the recommended control;

- legislation and regulatory requirements (both for and against);

- organisational policy;

- operational impact (is the control likely to have a negative effect on the operational capacity of resources?);

- safety and reliability.

ISO13335-3 (now replaced by ISO27005, which includes the same material – but less clearly set out – at clause 9.2) suggested that there are six constraints that should be considered when selecting controls:

- **Time constraints:** controls should be capable of implementation within an acceptable timescale, in relation to both the lifetime of the system and the period of exposure to the risk.

- **Financial constraints:** control implementations should be carried out within the set budget and the constraints of the cost-benefit analysis.

- **Technical constraints:** issues such as the compatibility of programs, software and hardware have to be taken into account.

- **Cultural or sociological constraints:** the active support of staff for a control is usually essential and if, therefore, staff do not understand or support a control decision, it is unlikely to be effective.

- **Environmental constraints:** space availability, climatic conditions, geography, and so on, can all influence the selection of controls.

- **Legal constraints:** legal factors, such as data protection or privacy requirements, may restrict the selection of controls, as could HR regulations and other laws.

ISO27005 identifies, in addition to the above:

- ethical constraints;
- ease of use;
- personnel constraints;
- constraints for integrating new and existing controls.

It provides no guidance on why these might be constraints.

It is not possible to provide total security against every single risk. It *is* possible to provide effective security against most risks, but the risks can change and so the process of reviewing and assessing risks and controls is an essential, ongoing one.

At clause 4.2.1 - g, ISO27001 requires the organisation to select appropriate control objectives and controls from those specified in Annex A, and requires this selection to be justified. However, it clearly invites organisations to approach this exhaustively and says, quite clearly, that additional controls may also be selected. ISO27001 auditors are likely to challenge implemented controls that are in excess of those required by the risk assessment on the basis that this may indicate inadequate controls applied elsewhere. ISO27002 provides good practice on each of the listed controls. There are, however, some areas in which organisations may need to go further than is specified in either standard and the extent to which this may be necessary is driven by the extent to which technology and threats have evolved since the publication of both standards.

It may also be that the organisation needs, in the light of its risk assessment, to implement controls other than those listed in Annex A. It might, for instance, have specialist processes that require additional security measures, or highly sensitive equipment that needs added protection. Additional controls can be added to the 133 that are already listed in Annex A. It would be sensible for an organisation that is adding controls to choose them from a reputable source (and to document the reasons for the choice), such as the hardware or software vendor (e.g. Microsoft or CISCO),

NIST,[51] the ISF,[52] COBIT[53] or some other source of good practice guidance.

Controls are selected in the light of a control objective. A control objective is a statement of an organisation's intent to control some part of its processes or assets and what it intends to achieve through application of the control. The cost of implementing (in cash and resource deployment) each control should not exceed the potential impact (assessed in line with the guidance in Chapter 6) of the risks (including safety, personal information, legal and regulatory obligations, image and reputation) it is designed to reduce.

It is important that, when considering controls, the likely security incidents that need to be detected should be considered and planned for. Clause 4.2.2 - h of the standard requires the implementation of controls that will enable 'prompt detection of and response to security incidents'. In effect, the process of selecting individual controls from those listed in Annex A should also include consideration of what evidence – measures of effectiveness[54] – will be required:

- to demonstrate that the control has been implemented and is working effectively; and

---

[51] The US National Institute of Standards and Technology has a specialist Computer Security Resource Centre with many highly important information security resources: *http://csrc.nist.gov*.

[52] The Information Security Forum is a private, members-only group with high membership fees, at: *www.securityforum.org*.

[53] Control Objectives for Information and Related Technology, available from ISACA: *www.isaca.org*.

[54] There will be a separate title in the ITGP 'Implementing ISO27001' series that specifically covers measures of effectiveness.

- that each risk has, thereby, been reduced to an acceptable level, as required by clause 4.2.1 of the standard. In other words, controls must be constructed in such a manner that any error, or failure during their execution, is capable of prompt detection and that planned corrective action, whether automated or manual, is effective in reducing the risk of whatever may happen next to an acceptable level.

Annex A of ISO27001 has 11 major categories, each of which has a number of subsections. There are, in total, 133 sub-clauses, each of which has a four-character alpha-numeric clause number. Each of these is a control under ISO27001 and each needs to be considered and a decision made as to whether or not it is applicable. The outcome of that decision is recorded in the Statement of Applicability, which is described in the next chapter.

The application of a control should reduce the risk it is designed to address. It will not always reduce that risk below the acceptable risk level. In this case, additional controls must be selected and applied until the cumulative effect of the controls is to reduce the identified risk below that acceptable risk threshold. The principle of not investing more on controlling a risk continues to apply as the size of the risk is reduced by the application of successive controls. It is, in other words, worth remembering that each additional control that is applied, is applied to a reduced risk level and that, therefore, it would be inappropriate to invest as much in the subsequent controls as in the initial one.

Risk assessment and existing controls

ISO27001 says that the risk assessment should 'assess the realistic likelihood of security failures occurring in the light of prevailing threats and vulnerabilities, and impacts associated with these assets, and *the controls currently implemented'.*[55] Whilst this is obviously the correct approach for second and subsequent risk assessments, it is not terribly helpful in respect of the initial risk assessment, in that it assumes that all the controls which have already been applied, usually without the benefit of a structured risk assessment, are appropriate controls for the identified risk.

In fact, it is quite often the case that, in the course of an ISO27001 risk assessment, organisations discover that some of their controls are in excess of their requirements and can be reduced; the consequent savings benefit the bottom line or enable deployment of other controls needed elsewhere.

The logical approach (which should be reflected in your methodology and, therefore, in your choice of risk assessment tool) is, as we indicated earlier, for the initial risk assessment to take place only after identifying the existing controls. It makes sense, in other words, to identify all existing controls that are applied to each asset at the point of identifying the assets and then carrying out the initial risk assessment and then potentially do both a 'before' and an 'after' assessment.

You should easily be able to identify, in the 'after' assessment, those assets which you have 'over-controlled' by the fact that, in comparison to the 'before' assessment,

---

[55] ISO27001 clause 4.2.1 - e2.

the 'after' assessed risk level is very close to zero (i.e. well within the risk acceptance criteria) and where the removal or reduction of controls would not necessarily move the risk out beyond the level of risk tolerance.

This approach will enable you to link your risk treatment plan (*see Chapter 15*) directly to the risk assessment, insofar as you will be able to identify that, for some risks, no further action is necessary whereas, for others, controls will either be implemented or dismantled.

Some refer to risk levels calculated ignoring the effect of any controls that may be in place as the 'gross risk' and those that are estimated in light of the prescribed controls as 'net risk'. Note that the Statement of Applicability should identify the controls required by the 'before' assessment and should, therefore, reflect all the controls applied.

Residual risk

Whatever risk is left after all selected controls have been applied is known as 'residual risk'. In most cases, this residual risk will be below the acceptable threshold and, therefore, obtaining management's approval (prior to implementation) should be a formality.

There will be circumstances where it has not been possible to reduce risk below the acceptable level (where, for instance, the cost of implementing an appropriate control is much greater than the impact value of the remaining risk that is outside the risk tolerance level) and this residual risk must also be explicitly signed off as acceptable by management.

Risks can, as we've said before, never be reduced to zero, even with the largest security budget. The possibility that one of the attributes of information security (i.e. confidentiality, integrity and availability) will be compromised will always exist. Prescribing additional measures will, of course, incur extra cost, and will offer diminishing returns in terms of increased information security. This is where the fourth option for treating information security risks comes in.

Risk transfer

Most organisations will at least consider transferring some of the risk or, rather, reducing the impact of some risks by transferring them to a third party via insurance. The aim here is to limit the potential financial losses by obtaining protective cover at a reasonable cost.

Insurance can be purchased to cover most risks. It is vital to ensure that any insurance you purchase matches the exact needs and risks identified. Buying inadequate cover, whether an inappropriate amount or for the wrong circumstance, will leave an unacceptable level of residual risk that may only be identified when it is too late.

In addition to the traditional insurance policies, specialised policies addressing information security risks are becoming more widely available. Underwriters can be found for all types of insurance needs, with sufficient shopping around.

Marrying suitable arrangements to transfer risks with risk control and avoidance policies can provide a risk strategy that meets organisational needs. Suitable implementation and monitoring result in a residual risk that reflects the organisation's risk appetite.

Risk transfer, though, is not the same as risk avoidance. When transferring risk, the ultimate accountability for that risk still rests with the transferor. If, for instance, the transferee insurance company refuses to pay, or becomes insolvent, the transferor will still bear the full impact of the risk. It is important, therefore, that the effectiveness of risk transference strategies is reviewed on a regular basis; risk transfer policies should be subject to testing in just the same way as are business continuity plans.

Optimising the solution

There is a lot of benefit to preparing a cost-benefit analysis for the Risk Treatment Plan, which itself will be further discussed in Chapter 15. A cost-benefit analysis could also be a sensible step in the 'plan' phase for all future control decisions, for proposed new controls or for enhanced controls. It would encompass the following:

- determining the impact of implementing the new or enhanced controls;

- determining the impact of *not* implementing the new or enhanced controls;

- estimating the total costs of the implementation. These should include all those components that your organisation routinely uses to calculate total cost of ownership (TCO) and may include, but are not limited to:

  - hardware and software purchases;
  - reduced operational effectiveness if system performance or functionality is reduced as a result of increased security;
  - cost of implementing additional policies and procedures;

- cost of hiring additional personnel to implement proposed policies, procedures or services;
- training costs; and
- maintenance costs.

A cost-benefit analysis, carried out at the point of selecting controls, enables the organisation to select those controls that will deliver most security enhancement for the lowest total cost, and will provide the basis for driving future improvements through the ISMS.

CHAPTER 14: THE STATEMENT OF APPLICABILITY

Having conducted the risk assessment and taken decisions regarding the treatment of those assessed risks, the results need to be documented. This produces two documents:

- Statement of Applicability, and

- Risk Treatment Plan.

The first lists all the controls listed in Annex A of ISO27001 and documents whether or not they have been applied within the ISMS, and also identifies additional controls that have been applied. The second maps the selected treatments (and the measures by which they are to be implemented) to the specific risks they are intended to address and is, in effect, a control implementation plan; we discuss this further in Chapter 15.

Drafting the Statement of Applicability

As the controls are selected, the Statement of Applicability (SoA) can start being drawn up. This SoA (specified in 4.2.1 - h of the standard) is documentation of the decisions reached on each control in light of the risk assessment and is also an explanation or justification of why any controls that are listed in Annex A have not been selected.[56] This exercise, of reviewing the list of controls and documenting

---

[56] ISO27001 clause 4.2.1 - j3.

the reasons for excluding any that have not been selected, is a useful cross-check on the control selection process.

The SoA needs to be reviewed on a defined, regular basis and will be one of the first documents that an external auditor will want to see. It is also the document that is used to demonstrate to third parties the degree of security that has been implemented and is referred to, with its issue status, in the certificate of compliance issued by third party certification bodies.

The SoA could adopt the format set out in the example below, in which the wording provided in the standard is repeated with appropriate variations to reflect the actual decisions made by the management steering group and its reasoning. The SoA can also refer to other documents, where these form the basis for any specific decisions recorded in it.

There are different ways of expressing the way in which different controls are applied, some of which are shown below. The SoA should be signed by the owner of the security domain for which it has been drawn up. This document is, for the external certification auditor, key evidence of the steps taken between risk assessment and implementation of appropriate controls; it often contains references to the parts of the ISMS which enforce or implement those controls.

Introduction

This is the Statement of Applicability, as specified in clause 4.2.1.h to ISO27001:2005 ('the Standard'), for ABC Ltd. It was adopted by the Management Steering Group on [date] and will be reviewed in the light of significant information security incidents and at least annually. It reflects a risk assessment carried out on [date]. Controls are addressed in the same order and using the same numbering as in Annex A of the Standard and this statement explains which controls have been adopted, and identifies those which have not been adopted and sets out the reasons for these decisions.

Statement of Applicability

A.5.1.1 Information Security Policy

ABC Ltd approved an Information Security Policy that conforms to the guidance of ISO27002:2005 on [date] and has published and communicated it to all employees and relevant external parties.

A.6.1.1 Management commitment to information security

ABC Ltd has established an Information Security Steering Group, that reports to the CEO, and which includes representatives from all the key parts of the organisation. This group approved – and is responsible for regular reviews to – the Information Security Policy and is responsible for assigning and/or resourcing security roles within the organisation, and for driving and reviewing implementation across the organisation of the ISMS and any individual initiatives, including information security training and awareness. An external information security adviser has been contracted to provide specialist advice as well as ongoing expertise to the Steering Group.

A.6.1.2 The Steering Group

The Steering Group provides a cross-functional forum within which representatives from key parts of the organisation are able to coordinate implementation of the complete range of information security controls. A separate forum for information security coordination has not been created as it is considered more effective for this to be handled through the management Steering Group.

[Through all controls, e.g.]

A.9.2.1 Equipment siting and protection

In each situation where there is a possibility that sensitive information might be overseen, a risk assessment is carried out and the appropriate controls, as identified in this section, are applied.

[Or]

A.10.8.4   Physical media in transit

This control has not been adopted, as ABC's physical media never leaves its premises.

This book does not explore each of the controls specified under Annex A, as those are addressed elsewhere.[57]

The Statement of Applicability will also list those additional controls that the organisation has determined, following its risk assessment, are necessary to counter specifically identified risks. These controls should be listed, either within those control sections whose objectives are supported by the additional controls, or within additional control sections added after those contained in ISO27001 Appendix A. These additional controls should adopt the Appendix A numbering scheme. It would also be worth documenting how the additional controls were selected.

It is sometimes argued that an organisation's Statement of Applicability should not be made available to anyone outside the organisation and, possibly, even subjected to restricted accessibility within it. However, given that the ISO27001 accredited certificate will explicitly recognise the Statement of Applicability document and version number it is reasonable to expect that those looking to examine the degree of assurance your organisation's ISMS provides will

---

[57] See, for instance, *International IT Governance: An Executive Guide to ISO 27001/ISO 17799*, by Alan Calder and Steve G Watkins (Kogan Page, 2006), as well as the various books on ISO27001 series from IT Governance Publishing.

ask for sight of it. Of course, you could insist on them signing a non-disclosure agreement prior to granting them sight of the document. Alternatively, you could classify the document, or at least one version of it, as publicly available, with a different, more comprehensive version containing any sensitive information being given a tighter security classification.

CHAPTER 15: THE GAP ANALYSIS AND RISK TREATMENT PLAN

Whilst the Statement of Applicability identifies which of the ISO27001 Appendix A controls (and which, if any, additional controls) are to be implemented, it does not prioritise implementation or provide any guidance for how implementation is to be carried out.

Of course, it would be logical for the organisation to tackle and implement controls in the order of priority (i.e. 'very high' first) identified through the risk assessment. The controls that are most critical for the organisation will be those that relate to the threats and vulnerabilities that it has identified, through the risk assessment process, as being most serious to its most critical systems.

Gap analysis

The reality is that most organisations that set out to achieve ISO27001 certification already have a number of information security measures in place and we touched, in Chapter 13, on the requirement to identify and record the original controls when doing the initial risk assessment. ISO27001 necessitates ensuring that those controls that are in place are adequate and appropriate and that additional required controls are implemented as quickly as possible. In other words, although the standard does not explicitly require one, an analysis of the gap between what is in place and what is required following the risk assessment should be carried out.

This gap analysis can be conducted either bottom-up or top-down. A bottom-up analysis will start with the information gathered during the risk assessment process, about all controls currently in place inside the organisation, and then assess whether or not they are adequate against the requirements of the organisation's Statement of Applicability and the standard. A top-down approach starts with the controls identified in the Statement of Applicability and assesses, by comparison with the existing controls, the extent to which the new requirements have already been met. The authors' preferred approach is the top-down one, as this will most quickly identify the critical loopholes in the existing security systems, as well as the controls that are unnecessary and can be eliminated or limited.

The Statement of Applicability will be complete once all the identified risks have been assessed and the applicability of all the identified controls has been considered and documented. Usually, the statement is started before any controls are implemented and completed as the final control is put in place.

The gap analysis is really the essential step in the creation of the Risk Treatment Plan and, when compared to the original 'benchmark starting point', can act as a progress report.

Risk Treatment Plan

Clause 4.2.2 - a of the standard requires the organisation to 'formulate a risk treatment plan that identifies the appropriate management action, responsibilities and priorities for managing information security risks'. Risk treatment is, as we saw earlier, part of the risk management process.

There is a link to ISO27001 clause 5, a substantial clause dealing in detail with management responsibility. Clearly, the Risk Treatment Plan needs to be documented. It should be set within the context of the organisation's information security policy and it should clearly identify the organisation's approach to risk and its criteria for accepting risk, as discussed elsewhere in this book. The risk assessment process must be formally defined and responsibility for carrying it out, reviewing it and renewing it, formally allocated. At the heart of this plan is a detailed schedule, which shows for each identified asset:

- each threat-vulnerability relationship and the associated risk level (from the risk assessment tool);

- the gap between the assessed risk and the acceptable level of risk;

- how the organisation has decided to treat the risk (accept, reject, control, transfer);

- the control gap analysis:

  - what controls are already in place and their nature (e.g. deterrent, preventive, etc.);
  - what additional controls are considered necessary, and their nature (and details of any supporting cost-benefit analysis);

- the resources required for the task (financial, technical and human);

- the timeframe for implementing the controls.

The Risk Treatment Plan links the risk assessment (contained in the chosen risk assessment tool and its outputs) to the identification and design of appropriate controls, as described in the Statement of Applicability, such that the board-defined approach to risk is implemented, tested and improved. This plan should also ensure adequate funding and resources for implementation of the selected controls and should set out clearly what these are.

The Risk Treatment Plan should also identify the individual competence and broader training and awareness requirements necessary for its execution and continuous improvement.

We see the Risk Treatment Plan as the key document that links both components of the risk management process and all four phases of the PDCA cycle for the ISMS. It is a high-level, documented identification of who is responsible for delivering which risk management objectives, of how this is to be done, with what resources, and how this is to be assessed and improved; but at its core is the detailed schedule describing who is responsible for taking what action, in respect of each risk, to bring it within acceptable levels.

CHAPTER 16: REPEATING AND REVIEWING THE RISK ASSESSMENT

Effective risk management is a continuous Plan-Do-Check-Act cycle. This means, of course, that the risk assessment must be regularly revisited. ISO27001 sets out the requirement very clearly: 'review risk assessments at planned intervals and review the residual risks and the identified acceptable levels of risks' taking into account changes in the business environment, to the organisation, to the risks it faces, to the incidents it experiences, to regulatory changes and in the light of the effectiveness of the controls.[58]

Following the initial, resource-intensive phase of the 'ISMS implementation' risk assessment, the organisation's appetite to repeat the exercise is likely to have diminished significantly. The real value in having done a comprehensively thorough risk assessment – using a tool that retains the data so that it can support future reviews – is that it enables you to achieve certification *and* you will be able to use it time and time again to review progress and ensure that the residual risk remains exactly where you want it – beneath the risk acceptance criteria.

Given the rate of development of new threats, the discovery of new vulnerabilities and the development of new technology (with its own inherent vulnerabilities), the information security management system needs to be continually reviewed to ensure it remains fit for purpose

---

[58] ISO27001, clause 4.2.3 - d.

and that it meets the requirements of the information security policy. To do this, the risk assessment needs to be reviewed.

Clause 4.2.3 - d of ISO27001 requires the organisation to 'review risk assessments at planned intervals and [to] review the residual risks and identified acceptable levels of risks', taking into account changes to the organisation and its business objectives, the risk environment (i.e. threats, vulnerabilities and likelihoods), the emergence of new technology and changing usage of existing systems, and changes to regulatory and compliance requirements.

There are two types of review: a review that takes place in response to a specific change of circumstances, such as a proposal to introduce a new technology, provide a new service or respond to a regulatory change; and a review that takes place on a regular basis and which considers the overall effectiveness of the controls that are currently in place. This regular review should take place at least annually in smaller businesses, but in larger organisations should probably be done on a rolling monthly schedule which ensures that the entire risk assessment is reviewed across the twelve month period.

Review(s) should be part of the overall management review of the ISMS and should look at the aggregated outputs of the incident reporting procedure as well as from the various processes put in place to measure[59] the effectiveness of controls (as required by clause 4.2.3 - c).

---

[59] For further guidance on this subject, see the Pocket Guide to ISO27004, due to be published by ITGP in 2010.

The standard describes the reviewing of the ISMS and risk assessment so as to make sure it continues to satisfactorily manage information security risks as 'continuous improvement'. The real benefit, though, of such a continuous improvement process is in the improved economy and effectiveness of the controls that address the identified risks (the latter being used to improve the return on information security investment, and hence, economy again).

The actual process of reviewing the risk assessment can be as straightforward as you wish: at the basic level, this would involve:

- formalising any changes to the organisation's risk management framework and risk acceptance criteria;

- identifying any changes to the information assets of the business which hadn't already been recorded for risk assessment purposes;

- identifying any previously unrecorded changes to the business, regulatory and contractual contexts;

- identifying any previously unrecorded changes to the risk environment (i.e. new or changed threats, vulnerabilities, likelihoods or impacts);

- identifying any resultant changes required to the risk treatment and control decisions;

- identifying any resultant changes to residual risk calculations and, if there is an increase in residual risk, obtaining formal approval for it; and

- ensuring that the process is fully documented.

APPENDIX 1: CARRYING OUT AN ISO27001 RISK ASSESSMENT USING vsRISK™

As we've said in this book, risk assessment is a *core competence* for information security management. We've also said that, without using a database risk assessment tool, it is virtually impossible to adequately manage an ISO27001-compliant information security risk assessment in any organisation that has more than a handful of staff and very few information assets. This appendix builds on the content of this book to guide the reader through the process of selecting a risk assessment tool and carrying out an ISO27001-compliant risk assessment in line with the requirements of ISO27001 4.2.1 - c to j using that tool.

In this book, we have recommended vsRisk™, and our reasons for doing so are contained in Chapter 5. This appendix complements that chapter.

If you wish to purchase a copy of vsRisk™, here is a link:

www.itgovernance.co.uk/products/744.

Here is a link for the information security risk management standard, BS7799-3:2006:

www.itgovernance.co.uk/products/162.

How the tool actually works

- vsRisk™ is loaded directly onto a workstation or the Information Security Manager's laptop.

- Before use, vsRisk™ is configured appropriately. In the Introductory section of the tool, the name and contact details for the Lead Risk Assessor are loaded. This is the person who, in line with the requirements of ISO27001 clause 7.1, is the owner of this asset. A user name and password (selected in line with company policy) are loaded into the next screen.

- In the next section (ISMS Scope/Policy) of vsRisk™ type in the first box (Scope) a reference to the document containing the scope statement, together with the interfaces and dependencies therein defined that limit the scope of the ISMS. Type in the second box (Policy Objective) the reference to the final version of the risk management framework objectives. It is possible, once configuration is complete, to upload the full version of both these documents to the tool, although a duplicate needs to be maintained for wider access through your ISMS and so it is advised that in vsRisk™ you record references to where the latest, current version of each ISMS document can be found.

- In the next configuration section (Classification Labels), enter the classification levels that you have selected as required by clause 7.2 of the standard. Note that, in the absence of a positive input, it will default to the basic levels outlined in *International IT Governance: An Executive Guide ISO27001/ISO17799*, which are 'private, restricted, confidential and public'. They can be changed later, if required.

- In the next configuration section (Management scale), input the scales that you have decided to use, both of which should be documented in your risk management framework. Both the impact valuation scale and the likelihood level scale can have between three and seven levels.

- The risk level matrix will then be produced automatically by the vsRisk™ tool, using a multi-level scale that takes account of both extent of impact and frequency of occurrence.

- In the next configuration section (Risk Acceptance Criteria), use the slider to enter the acceptable risk criteria that were defined in your risk management framework. Acceptable levels of risk are defined as those that are the same as, or below, the board-approved acceptable risk level. 'Acceptable risk' is defined as any risk that falls into a defined level between one and ten in the risk matrix calculated in vsRisk™. (The maximum value may be less than ten, depending on the scales you have selected for likelihood and impact.)

- Note that although the decision as to risk assessment criteria can be changed at a later date, it will possibly render invalid all the risk treatment decisions made prior to the change. You should, therefore, require any changes to the risk acceptance criteria to be formally approved before any changes are made.

- You will then be presented with a screen that enables you to confirm all the input data; confirm and you will be passed to the vsRisk™ login screen.

Training requirements

- The vsRisk™ training requirements are limited.

- vsRisk™ has detailed onscreen guidance. The Lead Risk Assessor is required to familiarise himself/herself with the principles of ISO27001 risk management and is then required to read the vsRisk™ overview that is provided

- Users other than the Lead Risk Assessor can be guided, as appropriate, by the Lead Risk Assessor. Once the user is clear about how each vsRisk™ step should be carried out, the risk assessment itself can begin.

Start using vsRisk™ for your risk assessment

Help instructions in vsRisk™ should be consulted and take priority over any variations with the instructions here, until such time as these instructions are issued within your applicable ISMS.

Identify the assets

- The assets that are within the scope of the ISMS, together with their owners, are identified by the asset owners and placed within asset groups. Asset owners are responsible for loading details of their assets, by asset group, into vsRisk™, either directly through the tool itself or through the vsAsset Monitor, which is a data collection module supplied with the tool.

- The organisation maintains a single inventory of information assets, which is subdivided by information asset owner into separate asset groups (which include assets grouped into systems, as explained below) within vsRisk™. Asset groups are required and are easily created in vsRisk™. Each asset is also classified as:

- hardware (all computing and information processing equipment, including printers, fax machines, photocopiers, etc.);
- software;
- IP;
- information/database (e.g. customer database, sales records, accounting ledgers);
- service, which includes designated secure areas;
- people (those individuals whose skills, knowledge and experience are considered essential);
- intangibles;
- processes; and
- other assets.

- For each asset, the organisation identifies the business unit or business role that 'owns' the asset. For software, the owner is its trained system administrator. The owner is responsible for: ensuring that the asset is correctly classified within vsRisk™; using the sensitivity/ classification labels that are contained there (and which are the same as those adopted by the organisation); day-to-day maintenance of the identified controls; and ensuring that access controls are defined and periodically reviewed, and that vulnerabilities are identified and patched. The details of each identified asset owner are loaded into vsRisk™.

- The organisation may group some assets together into composite information 'systems', in which case it identifies the assets within the system and the owner is the business unit or role responsible for the system.

- Assets are now added to vsRisk™.

- For each asset, the asset owner either enters directly into the vsRisk™ asset screen (by adding to a group, or by adding to an asset owner) and then completes the fields provided there for asset details, or uses the vsMonitor to provide asset details to the Risk Assessor, as instructed by the Information Security Manager. The business, contractual and legal/regulatory requirements are added, for each asset, using the free text boxes in the asset entry screen. Each asset also has its asset type and classification marked, using vsRisk™ drop-down lists, when the asset details are entered.

- Details about existing controls are added by selection from the Annex A list of controls.

- All new information assets are added to vsRisk™ as and when they are acquired, together with details of their requirements and values, and removed from the schedule when they are disposed of, as the standard requires.

- When new information assets are acquired, or existing assets in any way changed, those assets are added to the vsRisk™ inventory and are treated in line with the requirements below.

Identify the risks

- The vsRisk™ Risk Assessment Wizard is used to carry out the risk identification and treatment decision stages of the risk assessment.

- The first step is to input, using the qualitative scale defined in your risk management framework, the asset value; this is the maximum potential loss to the organisation estimated for each of confidentiality, availability and integrity for each of business, legal/regulatory and contractual (unless your organisation has opted to batch these together and use only one set of values for confidentiality, integrity and availability – this will be determined by the methodology you embrace and communicated via the document describing the risk assessment methodology). Choose the 'Assessments' tab from the top central menu and then click on the individual asset to bring up the 'Assessments Overview' page. For each of the asset attributes, select the 'Edit' option, use the sliding scale to identify the value, provide a full text justification for the decision, and 'Save'.

- The threats to each of the assets are identified by the asset owners, initially by consideration of the threats listed in the vsRisk™ Threat Database, and secondly, by consideration of threats that might not be in the database and which the asset owner is responsible for adding. Threats are considered for each of the three attributes of availability, confidentiality and integrity and for each of the business, legal/regulatory and contractual requirements of the asset.

- The asset owner is responsible for identifying the vulnerabilities that might be exploited by each of these threats, initially by consideration of the vulnerabilities listed in the vsRisk™ Vulnerability Database, and secondly, by consideration of vulnerabilities that might not be in the database and which the asset owner is responsible for adding.

- Where new vulnerabilities or weaknesses are identified (e.g. through the information security event reporting procedure), the Vulnerability Database is updated and, if appropriate, the risk assessment procedure set out here is repeated and any changed controls implemented.

Assess the risks

- The impact that might result from each threat-vulnerability is defined, as part of the risk assessment methodology, as the value of the asset the threat-vulnerability combination would exploit and this figure is held for each attribute within vsRisk™.

- The realistic likelihood that each of these failures might occur is assessed using the likelihood scale set out in the Risk Management Framework, and easily configured using the vsRisk™ sliding scale.

- The risk levels are then automatically calculated, for each risk, by vsRisk™ and shown in the 'Risk Rating' column for that asset.

Identify and evaluate options for the treatment of risks

- The vsRisk™ tool then uses the customised risk acceptance criteria (configured as set out above and in line with the requirements of the Risk Management Framework) to make a recommendation, for each of the assessed risks, as to risk treatment and whether the risk is acceptable (in which case vsRisk™ will indicate that no further action is required) or whether it must be controlled in line with the previously established criteria.

Select control objectives and controls for treatment of the risks

- Appropriate control objectives and controls are selected from those listed in the vsRisk™ Controls Database (which contains all the control objectives and controls from Annex A of ISO27001).

- If the Controls Database is inadequate in respect of controls for specific risks, then the Lead Risk Assessor will authorise the import, through the 'Administration' section of vsRisk™, of additional controls, which can then be selected to treat that risk.

- Once a control has been selected, the Risk Assessment Wizard will require the Assessor to estimate the extent to which the selected control will reduce impact and/or likelihood by adjusting the slide controls, and the tool will then automatically calculate the residual risk. If the residual risk is greater than the authorised risk acceptance criteria the Risk Assessment Wizard will provide the opportunity to repeat the control selection process continuously until the risk is level with or lower than the risk appetite. Once the residual risk is at or below the risk acceptance criteria, vsRisk™ will not require further action.

- The final residual risk will then be shown in the risk assessment table for the threat-vulnerability combination. You can also print out, from the 'Report Generator', a report summarising residual risk, for the board to authorise, as required by the standard.

- vsRisk™ will then summarise all the existing and selected control objectives and controls for the Statement of Applicability, which can then be drawn up together with the justification for accepting/rejecting each ISO27001 control, using the Statement of Applicability (SoA) Report Generating Wizard, as required. The SoA is then authorised by the board.

• The Statement of Applicability and the Asset Risk Report can then be used to inform the organisation's risk treatment plan.

APPENDIX 2: ISO27001 IMPLEMENTATION RESOURCES

Information and advice

www.itgovernance.co.uk/iso27001.aspx

Certification bodies and other organisations

www.itgovernance.co.uk/web_links.aspx

vsRisk™

www.itgovernance.co.uk/products/744

The Documentation Toolkit

www.itgovernance.co.uk/products/36

Try before you buy:

www.itgovernance.co.uk/free_trial.aspx

Information security standards ISO27001, ISO27002, ISO27005 and BS7799-3

www.itgovernance.co.uk/standards.aspx

ISO27001 consultancy

www.itgovernance.co.uk/iso27001_consultancy.aspx

Appendix 2:ISO27001 Implementation Resources

ISO27001 training courses
www.itgovernance.co.uk/iso27001_training.aspx

ISO27001 implementation manuals from ITGP

- *Application Security in the ISO27001 Environment www.itgovernance.co.uk/products/1496*

- *ISO27001 in a Windows® Environment www.itgovernance.co.uk/products/2207*

- *Information Security Breaches: Avoidance and Treatment based on ISO27001 www.itgovernance.co.uk/products/2804*

- *Information Security Law: The Emerging Standard for Corporate Compliance www.itgovernance.co.uk/products/1976*

- *ISO27001/ISO27002: A Pocket Guide www.itgovernance.co.uk/products/2020*

- *Nine Steps to Success: an ISO27001 Implementation Overview www.itgovernance.co.uk/products/178*

- *Risk Assessment for Asset Owners www.itgovernance.co.uk/products/886*

- *The Case for ISO27001 www.itgovernance.co.uk/products/177*

BOOKS BY THE SAME AUTHORS

Books by Alan Calder and Steve G Watkins

IT Governance: A Manager's Guide to Data Security and ISO27001/ISO 27002 - 4th Edition, Alan Calder and Steve G Watkins (published by Kogan Page, 2005) *www.itgovernance.co.uk/products/4*

International IT Governance: An Executive Guide to ISO 17799/ISO 27001, Alan Calder and Steve G Watkins (published by Kogan Page, 2006) *www.itgovernance.co.uk/products/474*

ISO27000 and Information Security: A Combined Glossary, Alan Calder and Steve G Watkins (published by ITGP, 2010) *www.itgovernance.co.uk/products/748*

Books by Alan Calder

IT Governance: Implementing Frameworks and Standards for the Corporate Governance of IT, Alan Calder (published by ITGP, 2009)

IT Governance Today: A Practitioner's Handbook, Alan Calder (published by ITGP, 2005) *www.itgovernance.co.uk/products/18*

IT Governance: Guidelines for Directors, Alan Calder (published by ITGP, 2005) *www.itgovernance.co.uk/products/19*

Books by the Same Authors

The Case for ISO 27001, Alan Calder (published by ITGP, 2005)
www.itgovernance.co.uk/products/177

Nine Steps to Success: an ISO 27001 Implementation Overview, Alan Calder (published by ITGP, 2005)
www.itgovernance.co.uk/products/178

Information Security based on ISO 27001 and ISO 27002: A Management Guide, Alan Calder (published by Van Haren Publishing, 2009)
www.itgovernance.co.uk/products/344

Implementing Information Security based on ISO 27001 and ISO 27002: A Management Guide, Alan Calder (published by Van Haren Publishing, 2009)
www.itgovernance.co.uk/products/345

Books by Steve G Watkins

ISO27001 A Pocket Guide, Steve G Watkins (published by ITGP, 2007)
www.itgovernance.co.uk/products/729

ISO27001 Assessments Without Tears: A Pocket Guide, Steve G Watkins (published by ITGP, 2007)
www.itgovernance.co.uk/products/766

ITG RESOURCES

IT Governance Ltd. sources, creates and delivers products and services to meet the real-world, evolving IT governance needs of today's organisations, directors, managers and practitioners. The ITG website (*www.itgovernance.co.uk*) is the international one-stop-shop for corporate and IT governance information, advice, guidance, books, tools, training and consultancy.

http://www.itgovernance.co.uk/iso27001-risk-assessment.aspx is the information page from our website for information security risk management resources.

Other Websites

Books and tools published by IT Governance Publishing (ITGP) are available from all business booksellers and are also immediately available from the following websites:

www.itgovernance.co.uk/catalog/355 provides information and online purchasing facilities for every currently available book published by ITGP.

www.itgovernanceusa.com is a US$-based website that delivers the full range of IT Governance products to North America, and ships from within the continental US.

www.itgovernanceasia.com provides a selected range of ITGP products specifically for customers in South Asia.

www.27001.com is the IT Governance Ltd. website that deals specifically with information security management, and ships from within the continental US.

Pocket Guides

For full details of the entire range of pocket guides, simply follow the links at
www.itgovernance.co.uk/publishing.aspx.

Toolkits

ITG's unique range of toolkits includes the IT Governance Framework Toolkit, which contains all the tools and guidance that you will need in order to develop and implement an appropriate IT governance framework for your organisation. Full details can be found at
www.itgovernance.co.uk/ products/519.

For a free paper on how to use the proprietary Calder-Moir IT Governance Framework, and for a free trial version of the toolkit, see
www.itgovernance.co.uk/calder_moir.aspx.

There is also a wide range of toolkits to simplify implementation of management systems, such as an ISO/IEC 27001 ISMS or a BS25999 BCMS, and these can all be viewed and purchased online at
http://www.itgovernance.co.uk/catalog/1

Best Practice Reports

ITG's range of Best Practice Reports is now at *www.itgovernance.co.uk/best-practice-reports.aspx*. These offer you essential, pertinent, expertly researched information on an increasing number of key issues including Web 2.0 and Green IT.

Training and Consultancy

IT Governance also offers training and consultancy services across the entire spectrum of disciplines in the information governance arena. Details of training courses can be accessed at *www.itgovernance.co.uk/training.aspx* and descriptions of our consultancy services can be found at *http://www.itgovernance.co.uk/consulting.aspx*. Why not contact us to see how we could help you and your organisation?

Newsletter

IT governance is one of the hottest topics in business today, not least because it is also the fastest moving, so what better way to keep up than by subscribing to ITG's free monthly newsletter *Sentinel*? It provides monthly updates and resources across the whole spectrum of IT governance subject matter, including risk management, information security, ITIL and IT service management, project governance, compliance and so much more. Subscribe for your free copy at *www.itgovernance.co.uk/newsletter.aspx*.

Lightning Source UK Ltd.
Milton Keynes UK
UKOW06f0050250117
292821UK00001B/93/P

9 781849 280433